HOME
IS A
STRANGER

HOME
IS A
STRANGER

a Memoir

PARNAZ
FOROUTAN

AMBERJACK
PUBLISHING

CHICAGO

AMBERJACK
PUBLISHING

Amberjack Publishing
An imprint of Chicago Review Press Incorporated
814 North Franklin Street
Chicago, Illinois 60610

This memoir is a work of creative nonfiction. It is nonfiction in that this is a recounting of the author's memories, and creative in that the author has expanded on her memory to build a richer narrative. The events contained herein are accurate to the best of the author's memory. Names and minor details that do not impact the story have been changed as necessary to protect those involved.

Interior image reproduced with permission.

10 9 8 7 6 5 4 3 2 1

Book design by Aubrey Khan, Neuwirth & Associates

Library of Congress Cataloging-in-Publication Data
Is available from the Library of Congress

ISBN 978-1-948705-60-8
eBook ISBN 978-1-948705-61-5

To the friend G.d sent me,
in the darkest and loneliest hour of my need

A thousand years ago in Nishapur, a poet drew a map for the journey of the soul. A seeker, he wrote, travels through seven valleys. In the first valley, he comes to a place of questions, of uncertainties. In the second valley, he finds himself in the bewilderment of love. In the third, he comes to understand that he does not understand anything. In the fourth, he abandons his attachments to the world. In the fifth, he sees that all things are connected by love, and beyond all things, the Beloved. In the sixth valley, the wayfarer loses himself to wonder, to awe, and in this state, he enters the final valley, where he becomes timeless, placeless, annihilated.

Dear Father,

I am sitting at my writing desk, looking out the window at my garden in the morning light. There had been a drought for years. Then, this year, a fire burned through our town. Burned the ancient oaks, burned homes, charred the mountains black. It was followed by a deluge of rain, which was followed by a deluge of wildflowers and, now, a thousand butterflies in their migration pass by my window, all flying in the same direction, tumbling on the breeze.

You died on a morning like this, the first of May, twenty-two years ago. I was just a girl then. I could still feel you in the sunlight on my skin. I believed that if I listened closely enough, I could hear you laughing. I knew you had become the migration of butterflies, the seed, the blossom, the wilting, the mountain, the wind, the stone, the sea. I knew with certainty. So I threw myself into the world, searching for you in cities, in forests, on mountains, in music, through strangers.

I am no longer that girl, Father. I've lost her, you see? I awoke one morning and knew that she was gone. And she took with her all her certainties.

In the last year of your life, you lost the ability to speak. I spend my days searching for words. Outside my window, the migration of a thousand butterflies and foolishly, desperately, I write *Hills. Wildflowers. Breeze.*

Dear Father,

You died on a morning much like this. I awoke that day, and the beauty of the world devastated me. Now, I write so that I can hold it, for a moment, on this page, before it is all taken from me.

HOME
IS A
STRANGER

T he girls in our boat undressed and jumped into the sea. And I stood there, in my red bikini, considering death. In my dreams, death was always a tremendous amount of water, a flood, a tidal wave, a rushing torrent. In that weathered boat, while the rest of the party swam and squealed and ducked and dove beneath the surface, I kept looking at that bottomless expanse of it all until I heard the fisherman say, "Go ahead. Jump."

His job was not to talk to me, but to scan the horizon for patrol boats and, if he saw one, to give a sharp whistle to call us back into our respective boats. The boys would climb into theirs, and we girls would scramble into ours, to pull our hijabs over our wet bodies and veil our dripping hair and sit in pious contemplation of the blue and the horizon.

He sat there, leaning back, cigarette in hand, watching me.

"I'm not a good swimmer," I said.

"I am," the fisherman said. "Stay close to the boat. I'll keep an eye on you."

So I jumped.

I was suspended in the silent blue of it. There loomed the threat of being discovered by the police. But beneath the water, nobody could see me. I surfaced, gasped, looked at the boat, which seemed a little farther than I had expected. Then I went under, again. Eyes open. I turned and turned, weightless. It felt exhilarating to be in the waters of the Caspian with the bottom so deep, in Iran, with home so far away. I felt so brave, so alive. I surfaced again. I turned to find the boats and saw that everyone was scrambling in. Someone was calling my name above the deafening lull of the water. My cousin Javid waved at me frantically.

I swam over as fast as I could, the waves working against me. My arms felt leaden. I dragged myself through that water, terrified, frantic. Back in Los Angeles, I had heard about the dark prison cells, the beatings, the disappearances. I spent months worrying about these stories before I had made my decision to return to Iran. And was this moment it, my fate? I finally reached the boat and clutched the side and heaved myself up. The other girls were almost dressed, pulling their pants with panic over their wet legs, buttoning their manteaus with trembling fingers over their nearly bare breasts, tucking their dripping hair beneath knotted headscarves. I struggled clumsily with my jeans, shaking violently with fear. I was the only one still undressed. Then, the fisherman in our boat said, "It's okay. Don't be so afraid, it is just some local fishermen. They are not the police."

He waved at the distant boat. The men in it waved back. *It was a false alarm*, I thought, trying to steady myself, *I don't need to be covered in hijab. It is not the police.* I gave up trying to cover my wet body with my unwilling clothes, threw my jeans onto the bench and drew a deep breath as the boat came nearer.

Relieved that it wasn't the police and looking in the direction of that oncoming boat, I didn't see that behind me the other girls sat dressed in full hijab. The fishermen we had hired to take us out in their boats had just seen us in our bikinis, so I didn't register that before these other local fishermen, who were not paid to look away, we must be fully clothed. Maybe because of the sun, or the exhilaration of having been in the bottomless sea, or the close encounter with absolute terror, I forgot the codes of conduct in Iran, forgot that this wasn't Malibu or Venice, and the closer that boat came, the more distracted I was by this unforeseen situation to notice the bulging vein in Ali's neck, or the shock of the girls, or my male cousins' horror at my indiscretion. I stood there, hands shading my eyes from the sun, waiting to see what these strangers wanted, in the middle of the sea.

Javid said, from the other boat, in English, "Cover yourself up."

I didn't understand that he meant fully, in Islamic hijab. So I took my saffron silk headscarf and wrapped it about my torso, Tahitian style, the way I might have back home on the beaches of Southern California. I watched, mesmerized, the two older men who now stood in their boats before us, their faces wrinkled by the sun, their kind, curious, furtive eyes. They had thick mustaches, calloused hands. They wore knitted sweaters, wool caps on their heads, faded black pants, rubber boots with a tangled net at their feet. They turned off their motor and the three boats bobbed silently in the water. Then the older fishermen coughed, cleared their throats, and greeted the fishermen we had hired, barely glancing in the direction of the girls' boat where I stood. They turned to the boys' boat and asked if we wanted to buy their catch. They pointed to two large fish, gasping on the floor of their boat.

I was enraptured. It was such a magnificent exchange, so unexpected a meeting. Fishermen, in the middle of the sea, selling their catch. How could I have remembered what I was or was not wearing when I was no longer even cognizant of myself, lost to the newness of the experience? I had slipped beyond the veil, so to speak, of temporal reality. I thought to myself, *we, these older fishermen and I, are entities beyond the masks of our respective identities. We are the attraction of foreign, strange unknowns drawn together to learn, to understand, to make meaning.* However, what my cousins wanted to do was to end this transaction of meaning making as quickly as possible, so the younger one, Pouya, asked the fishermen how much for the fish and that's when I saw it. The third fish. Tiny. Long. Strange, like a small dinosaur. I had never seen anything like it.

"That one?" I said, addressing one of the older fishermen.

He leaned over and picked it up and said, "A hatchling sturgeon. Too small to eat."

It was an ancient thing. Smooth ridges down its back like a mountain range. "I'd like to buy that one," I said.

"For what?" the older fisherman asked. "It is useless."

"Please. I will pay for it. If you don't need it, I want to return it to the sea."

Maybe it was the strangeness of the creature. Or its grotesque beauty. Or the fact that it was to be wasted, this living thing, caught accidentally and left to die in the bottom of a boat. I wanted to return it to the water, where it would swim off to grow into the behemoth that it was destined to become. "It is near dead," Javid said from the boys' boat, perhaps through clenched teeth. The moment froze like that. The girls in their full hijab aghast. The boys angry. The hired fishermen waiting, the hatchling sturgeon gasping. I stood in my red bikini immodestly covered by a breeze-blown silk scarf, in the middle of the Caspian Sea, unable to think beyond the moment before me. The kind, older fishermen. This unexpected occurrence in an unlikely location. The urgency of the dying fish.

"You can have it," the older fisherman said to me. He held it out to me, with his eyes cast down.

"Don't take it," Ali said in English, perhaps through clenched teeth.

We were all Ali's guests, staying at his seashore villa. He was my cousin Pouya's closest friend and had invited us as an excuse to get to know me better, before a formal pursuit. The moment froze, again. I didn't know what the trespass was, but I started to understand that I had done something terribly offensive, though against whom, I didn't know. Was it that I had encroached upon the natural hospitality of these people and placed this poor village fisherman in the uncomfortable position of offering me a free fish?

"Don't take it," Ali said, again in English.

The older fisherman held the fish out to me, glancing over at me, to see if I intended to take it from his hand. I looked at the fish he held. It was marvelous. Blue, silver, green, its strange pointed face, its smallness in relation to the potential of what it was meant to become. Then, the fisherman in our boat, the one who told me to jump, who had promised to keep his eyes on me, said, quietly, "Go on." I looked up at him,

standing there, looking intently at me, still smoking his cigarette. He nodded. "Go ahead," he said. "You're right. It
belongs back in the sea."

So I took the fish, carefully, from the weathered hands of
the old man holding it out to me. I held it for a moment, then
I bent over the ledge of that red boat and gently set the fish in
the sea. We all watched it in silence, expectantly. And it just
floated there. Then, as if awakening, it jumped clear into the
air, a flash of silver, a piece of lightning, before it fell back
into the water and swam at the surface for a fraction of a
second, the sun glistening on it, green, purple, blue, before it
disappeared.

After the fish incident, we returned to Ali's villa. On the
walk back, Javid explained to me, patiently, my error in not
realizing that the unpaid older fishermen should not have seen
me half nude. Javid believed that the mistake was innocent
enough on my behalf, and the incident seemed to have passed
without consequence. Ali, however, wasn't as forgiving. The
locals knew him. He had a reputation to protect, and my
behavior threatened his honor within that small community.
I should have known better, as an Iranian girl, to be more
protective of my modesty. "You are too unladylike," he said.
I found myself apologizing, trying to defend myself, to prove
to him my innocence, but he shook his head and walked away
from me.

That afternoon, we grilled the fish we had bought, listened
to music, and danced, while Ali ignored me. Then, one of the
other girls invited on that trip, Naghmeh, pulled me aside and
said, "Let's take a shower together." Both of us were covered

in sand and salt and tired from the outing. Naghmeh. Blond-haired, petite and large-hipped, with the devil in her eyes. She used to date Ali. She and I walked to the large room that served as a hammam. Beautiful hand-painted tiles on the walls and floors, and a copper showerhead in the center of the room, with nothing to enclose it. We undressed and washed our bodies. We were young and supple and beautiful in the steam and the fading light of that late afternoon. We talked and laughed, and she told me stories about Ali, who kept knocking on the hammam door asking what I was up to now, locked up in the shower with Naghmeh. Then, Naghmeh brought up the fisherman we had hired.

"Wasn't he beautiful?" she asked me.

She was right. He was beautiful. Long and lean and toned. Gold skinned. High cheekbones, eyes gold in the light. Sensuous mouth. Beautiful. "Imagine his bed," she said. "Sheets that smell like saltwater . . ."

"With grains of sand in it . . ."

"A collection of seashells on his windowsill . . ."

"A mosquito net hanging over the bed . . ."

"The taste of his skin . . ."

"His mouth . . ."

"The strength of his arms . . ."

"Would he play an instrument?"

"Guitar?"

"Flute?"

"Daf. But only when he is angry."

"On moonlit nights, he'd take you fishing."

"Teach you how to throw the net."

"And wait . . ."

This went on, this dangerous unfolding narrative we made of him. We named him the golden fisherman, and soon it was night and we kept weaving him from this thread of fantasy and desire until well past midnight. Tangled in our own story, we finally fell asleep.

I AWOKE THE next morning to find Javid about to leave the house. He and Ahmad, the fisherman hired to ferry the boys, had arranged the day before to meet so that Ahmad could take Javid to the fish markets, to the dark back of a store where a man sold black market sturgeon caviar in tins.

"Do you want to come with me?" Javid asked.

Hungry for adventure and story, I threw on my headscarf and pulled on my sneakers and ran out to the gravel road that ended in sand, where Ahmad was supposed to meet us. Ahmad was to lead us to the fish market, through its winding passageways, past merchants singing about their bream, their whitefish and kutum, past the plastic bins full of ice and fish, with their futile gills, the shock of their eyes, the mouths that opened and closed in agony. The grounds of that fish market would have been strewn with slippery silver scales, entrails, scattered rainbows, and I imagined having to step with haste, with cautious feet past all those bins, the fish in them flopping, dying as we followed Ahmad quickly, covertly, to a nondescript store, to the dark back, where a man waited with tins of sturgeon caviar. I walked with Javid down the gravel road toward the sea to find Ahmad, but I would never participate in that black-market exchange, because just as we reached the sand, a mule came trotting along the beach.

I remember little about the rider sitting on top, bouncing, but I do remember that mule clearly. A thick, red kilim on its back, with yellow and green tassels hanging from the decorative thing on its head, and blue turquoise stones and bells, just jingling and jangling as it trotted along the water. It stopped before us and the man on the mule said, "Ahmad is coming soon."

That mule was lovely. Big, intelligent eyes and decked out splendidly, like a little parade. It tossed its head and whinnied. *This is not a thing of Los Angeles*, I thought, looking into his eyes. *Never would a mule arrive, decorated with so much love, to deliver a message.* Then, the man muttered something close to the mule's ear, which twitched in response, before the two turned to ride away.

"Wait," I called out to the man, not ready for him to leave yet. He stopped. Not knowing what else to say, I asked, "Do you hire out your mule?"

Javid and the man stared at me.

"I've never ridden on a mule before," I said. "In fact, I can't ever remember even seeing a mule. I just thought it might be interesting, to experience, the coast . . . in such a traditional way." The man looked at Javid, because Javid, as a man, was my assumed custodian. It didn't matter if Javid was my brother or cousin or husband or even friend. He was a man and, as a young woman, I was his charge. By token of his gender, the man expected permission from Javid before even addressing me. Even though I had initiated the exchange, even though I intended to pay for the service.

After a moment's pause, Javid turned to the man and said, "She is from America." The man nodded, as though in understanding. Then, Javid turned to me and said, "Fine. I'll walk back and get the car. It is getting too late to walk to the fish market, anyway. I'll drive over with Ahmad. You ride the mule, then go directly back to Ali's." Money exchanged hands, and I found myself sitting on top of that mule, like a village bride. The man pulled the mule by a rope and I rode on top, imagining a procession of dafs and women ululating, though no sign of a groom. We turned to ride back and that's when I saw the fisherman, the golden one, walking toward us, dazzling in the morning light.

The man with the mule greeted him and they started to talk, so I assumed my paid ride had come to an end. I dismounted the mule, patted his head, and turned to walk back to Ali's villa, when I heard the golden fisherman ask, "Do you want a ride in my boat?"

I stopped. A second's hesitation. Then I looked at him and said, "No, thank you."

I turned back to walk immediately, as my cousin had instructed, to Ali's home, even though Javid and I were born only six months apart, back when Tehran still had discos and our dads wore bellbottoms and our moms wore miniskirts and we watched Bruce Lee movies together on Friday afternoons while sipping Coca Cola from glass bottles, while students met secretly and talked about freedom and democracy, while students disappeared and mothers wept and searched for their sons and daughters, waited outside prisons, wrote letters, prayed and prayed, before enough was enough and the students took to the streets and the Shah fled and the void he left behind a blackness filled, and the war began and the air raid sirens woke us from sleep and sent us running to dark basements, and murals of martyrs covered the walls of buildings left standing, while the rest were rubbled heaps of brick and mortar, steel and bone. My family escaped, and Javid's family stayed behind, so when Javid had said to go straight back after the mule ride, and the golden fisherman asked, "Do you want to ride in my boat?" I turned and said, "No, thank you," then started walking home, as my cousin had instructed me. I stopped there for a moment, looking down the road that led back to Ali's house, with him, the golden fisherman, behind me, and behind him the beautiful blue beckoning of death, and I thought to myself, *but how long do we live, really?*

I turned around again. I looked at the golden fisherman, magnificently real in the morning light. And while he kept talking to the guy with the mule, he looked back at me, too. So I marched up to him and asked, "How much? For the boat ride?" Just to set things straight. Just to make it clear that I was hiring him, to take me out in his boat, so that I could contemplate the sea and the horizon. That the day before, when I stood on the ledge of his boat, trembling, and he had said, *go ahead, jump,* meant nothing. That when he was the only one to see my anguish about the hatchling sturgeon and my uncertainty, it meant nothing. He had a boat. It was for hire. I was a tourist. I had American dollars. And nothing else existed between the transaction of all those concretes. No thread of desire, no story of longing.

The two men said goodbye, and the mule rode off with the jingle and the jangle. I stood there. And the golden fisherman stood before me. His little red boat with the word *Morvarid* painted in white on one side and *Pearl* on the other was just a way off, beached in the sand. He started walking toward his boat and I followed, thinking *danger, trespass, police, customs, sharia, laws, beating, disappearance, drowning,* all to the pounding rhythm of my heart. According to sharia law, an unmarried girl could not be alone with an unmarried man, unless he was mahram, her father, her brother, perhaps an uncle. Any rumor of anything to do with moral misconduct could lead a young woman to find herself in the hands of the law, at the mercy of an Islamic court that could sentence anything from whippings to death by stoning.

But I was twenty-four, on the green, lush, humid shores of the Caspian, and the boat was red, and the sea seemed endless, and the man before me, who happened to be a fisherman, a vocation so full of allusions, radiated with some burning light, and all of this was a transgression forbidden to me. I was trapped in an old, old story. And that story wasn't just about physical attraction, it was about a compulsion to step closer to what is forbidden, to look and touch and taste, to come to know, beyond the fear of what is not known. It wasn't crude or carnal longing that drew me to the golden fisherman, it was the possibility of something perfect in its manifestation to occur between him and I, an understanding that would come to shift and change us both. So for the sake of platonic inquiry, I stepped in his boat, and I sat down, and tightened my headscarf, and looked off at the sea with the air

of some foreign tourist hiring some local fisherman to take me
out in his hired boat to the middle of the waters where I could
meditate on whatever people meditated on when they return
to the land of their birth, before the bombs and the Sisters
and Brothers of Islam sent them running. He pushed the boat
into the water. He started the motor. I was getting farther and
farther from the shore. I could feel him behind me. Then, over
the loud machinery of that boat, I heard him ask, "Do you
want to drive my boat?"

Me? Drive a little red boat into the face of the exhilarating
unknown?

I turned to look at him and nodded. He stopped the boat
and I got up. He moved over on the bench, and I sat down
where he had sat. We waited like that, for moment, in silence,
until he nodded his head toward a lever and he said, "Just
turn that. The more you turn, the faster it goes." I turned it a
little, and we putt-putted forward. I turned a little more, and
we hit those waves with the boat jumping a little each time.
He put his hand next to mine on the lever, an inch of space
between our hands, and that empty space between his skin
and mine burned with atomic energy. He held the lever and
said, "Turn it this way to go right, and this way to go left. It
will be a smoother ride."

Then he looked down at my hand. And I looked down, too,
and saw that, brazenly, the sleeve of my manteau revealed my
naked wrist. Smooth, delicate, white. He looked up at me,
and I looked into his eyes and I saw the generations of men
and women, lineages of lovers, the flame of all those who
coupled to create him. Tall, beautiful, skin turned gold by the

summer sun, and eyes gold, too, shining with light. I looked at him, and the boundaries between us dissolved. Or expanded. Because through his eyes I understood something of the infinite. Something of what that desire is that brims over from the confines of our bodies.

In that timeless place, he reached out across the great aching chasm of separation, and he traced his finger along the revealed skin of my wrist. A touch. Barely.

Perhaps in fear of what he had done, or what he might do next, he removed his hand quickly and looked away. And I revved up that motor and took those waves head-on. No rights or lefts to smooth out the ride, just a rage to hit each wave, so that we flew for a moment, airborne, before the boat crashed back down and may have splintered into pieces. Then I turned back toward the shore, with the boat tilting to its side, and drove that thing into the sand, stumbled out, wet from the spray, panting, unaware of all the eyes that had seen. I walked, without looking back, past the women in their dark chadors sitting on picnic blankets, past the men standing with arms crossed, smoking cigarettes, past children building castles in the sand, to the road that led to Ali's villa. I opened the door to find them all sitting at the table, spreading caviar on pieces of toast. Javid turned and asked, "How was the mule ride?"

Naghmeh looked at me and knew. She knew, from the bewildered look in my eyes, that something wonderful had just happened. That, somehow, it involved the story we had spent an afternoon and a night creating. He wasn't just some hired fisherman anymore, just as the sea wasn't just the sea anymore, and the ride on that tasseled mule and where it led me was too marvelous to reduce to a simple response of, "The mule ride was lovely. What a pleasant way to explore the shore." But I did say those words, and Javid nodded, and Ali looked up from his toast, upset that I had hired a mule without his permission. Ali had invited me to his villa to see if I was worth pursuing, and the incident with the local fishermen, the red bikini, and that hatchling sturgeon had left a bitterness in his mouth, because he sat now, visibly irritated that I had left his home without him, gone into public, and either unwittingly or intentionally undermined his masculinity once more, in this small fishing village on the coast of the Caspian where he reigned king.

Naghmeh, with the devil in her eyes, asked Ali, "Will we go swimming again today?"

Ali looked between the two of us, searching for clues masked by our words, by our tone, by the glances between us, to discover if we intended to mock him, before he said, "You girls will go swimming after we eat. Javid, Pouya, and I will be waterskiing."

After breakfast, we returned to the beach where the boys climbed into their hired boat and the girls into ours. The two boats set off in opposite directions, this time Ahmad towing Ali on water skis. When our boat was far enough from the shore to be seen, the golden fisherman shut off his engine and anchored. The boys' boat zoomed in our radius, with Pouya in tow now. I was first among the girls to undress. I felt his eyes on me. My cheeks burned hot, my body on fire. I stepped on the ledge of his boat and jumped. Because the desire to quench that burning, the intensity of it, was greater than the fear of death. I swam in the sea, waited for the other girls to jump, and when they were all swimming, I swam back to his boat unnoticed, pulled myself up and flopped in, all wet, like a clumsy fish, and he sat there, looking at me with my limbs askew, in the bottom of his boat, trying to gather myself with some semblance of grace. He took a slow drag on his cigarette, blew out the smoke, and asked, "You're not afraid anymore?"

"No."

"Are you Ali's girl?"

"No. No, I'm not."

"You are not from here."

"No."

"Where do you come from?"

"Los Angeles."

"You were born there?"

"I moved there when I was a child."

"Why have you come back?"

"I lost my father a few years ago. I wanted to find something of him, here. You?"

"I have always been here, like my father and his father."

"You are a fisherman?"

"Like my father and his father," he said, then looked off at the endless expanse of the water. "This is my sea."

"Do you like being a fisherman?"

"It's hard in the winter," he said, looking at me. "The summers are easy, though. I rent out my boat to take you city kids out to swim. But the winters . . ." He held out his hands. Strong. Calloused. Beautiful. I wanted to reach out, to touch them, to feel the power of their grip. I didn't. Ali was swimming, and he noticed me.

"Come back in," he yelled from the water.

"I'm tired."

"Then let's leave."

"Go back in," the fisherman said quietly. "I want to watch you."

I threw myself into that water with the passion of a suicide. I swam shamelessly. To the brink of exhaustion, of nearly drowning. Until it was time to return to the seashore, to walk away from him. I spent that afternoon and evening whispering with Naghmeh. Ali had taken to ignoring me completely and turned his attentions to Bita, another one of the girls in our party. We spent the night with music and dance.

When I was a child, one of my favorite stories about Iran was the one my father told about his own childhood, when he fetched the bread, baked fresh each morning. He'd walk to the neighborhood bakery, buy that bread piping hot, wrapped in paper, and bring it back to his family before breakfast. So when I awoke on our last morning by the seashore, I decided to buy the bread for our breakfast from the local bakery.

"I'm going to buy bread," I told Ali, asleep on the couch.

He hoisted himself onto his elbow. "No. You are not," he said. "Don't you dare leave." Then he flopped back down to sleep.

I shut the door softly behind me, took a deep breath of that heavy, humid morning air, and set off to find the local bakery. I walked along a road encroached by a green and lush forest, beside a marsh teeming with lotus and egrets, turtles, kingfishers and frogs. The sun was just coming up and a blanket of heavy mist lifted from the trees. I walked with a bounce to my step, until along came a young man on a bicycle. He rode past me, very slowly. I knew that I needed to keep my eyes down, unless I intended to be inviting, but being alone on an empty road early in the morning seemed invitation enough, so he started circling me. He rode around and around me as I walked forward, his circles getting tighter, until, choked by the threat of his proximity, I stopped. He stopped, too, right in front of me. There wasn't a single living soul on that road, save him and me. My heart was beating so hard, my head was spinning. I looked directly at him and I asked, "Where is the bakery?"

Something shifted. Maybe the clarity of my intentions occurred to him, the simple, banal, human act of buying bread. He looked at me, puzzled, then softened and started to give me detailed directions to the closest bakery. "Take the main road," he told me. "You'll be safer."

When I found the bakery, a simple box of a building with a large window and a glowing tandoor inside tended by three or four sweating men, it wasn't open yet. I walked around the corner to sit and wait, and there before me, sitting in a field of green, tall grass, were more than fifty local women in floral print chadors, chatting and laughing, and dispersed among them chickens and geese pecking the earth and clucking.

Those women were so lovely, with their rosy cheeks and sparkling eyes, the vitality of their being. I wanted badly to be taken into their fold, to learn who they were and what they thought and how they lived each day. I walked to where they all sat on their haunches, talking, and I said, greeting all of them at once, "Good morning."

Everything stopped. Dead quiet. The women, young and old, all looked at me in silence. A second passed, two, eternity. Then, they all looked away and continued talking.

I stood there, embarrassed. Hurt. Was it my clothes, my accent, the way I stood? Surely they could tell I wasn't from their village, which made me another tourist from the city, but did they know that it wasn't even one of their cities, but a foreign city altogether? Did they see this lack of belonging in me? I wanted so badly to belong. I wanted so badly to sit among them. Wasn't that longing itself a passport in? I felt like I was on the playgrounds of my childhood, again, in the suburban neighborhood school of Los Angeles. Nobody wanted to sit beside me or talk to me. I was a foreigner. A stranger. Gharib. I didn't have the words to say, "Please, allow me to join you, I have something to give." Instead, I thought, *I'll just buy my bread and leave.*

So I walked back around to the window, stood where I imagined the line would begin, ready to wait for the baker to open for business. After ten minutes, a beefy man with a red face opened the window and, suddenly, from around the building, the women rushed to that window. They shoved and pushed me violently as they lined up in front of me, until I found myself standing at the very end of that line, flustered. I straightened my headscarf, which someone had pulled undone, and brushed off my manteau, and told myself, *No matter, I'm in no hurry.* But then a strange thing happened. The baker ignored the first woman standing at his window.

Instead, he came out of the door, walked past all the women to the back of the line where I stood, and asked, "How many sheets of bread would you like, Miss?"

I looked at him, and he looked back kindly. Then, I looked at the women who had pushed me to the end of the line, and they did not look back kindly, so I said, quietly, "Five sheets, please." The baker walked past all the women, back into the bakery, took five sheets of fresh, hot sangak, dusted them off, wrapped them in paper, walked out past the now glaring women, and handed them to me.

"Thank you," I said. "How much?"

"Don't worry about it."

"That's kind of you, but I can pay, please. How much?"

"Don't worry about it. You should leave now, though."

"But I have money, I'm not poor or something."

He looked at the women waiting in line. Then, he came in real close to me and whispered, very seriously, "Morvarid."

That word. Painted in white. On the side of that red boat.

"Go now," he said. "Leave quickly. Across the street there is a taxi waiting for you."

I took my bread and walked briskly to the other side of the street. The driver was already holding the door open. I got in, and he shut it and drove me back to Ali's without even asking me where I was headed.

We ate that bread. I didn't tell anyone about the incident with the village women and the baker. We packed our bags. I needed to see the golden fisherman again. The story between the two of us couldn't end like this, with a village scandal, uncertainties, unsaid goodbyes. I suggested one more boat ride before the long drive back to Tehran, and everyone agreed that it seemed like a fine way to end the trip, so we headed to the shore, all of us, to find the fishermen.

He was there, waiting. Ahmad, too. We piled wordlessly into our respective boats. Somehow the air seemed thicker. Everything had a heavier gravity about it, the way the atmosphere feels before a storm. Naghmeh sat at the front of the boat and I sat in the middle, keeping my eyes on the horizon, not daring to look at him. After we rode for a while, with the spray in our faces, in silence, I finally turned around and met his eyes. Then, he did a peculiar thing. He turned that boat in a complete, graceful circle.

The other girls squealed with delight. He stopped the boat and instructed the girls to stand up and move to sit on one side of the boat. When I got up to join them, he said, "No, you sit where you are." Then, he started the boat's engine and turned it in a full circle again, but this time, my side lifted up into the air, so that I was looking down on the girls, who were nearly touching the water with their backs. He looked at me, lifted up like that, with the sky above reeling and the cool water beneath and that little red boat just turning and turning in the waves. Then, he sped that boat straight out to sea, and the girls screamed with the exhilaration of the speed and the spray, and I sat quietly, watching him, and he looked back quietly, and he slowed the boat down and turned it again, and my body rose once more with my side of the boat, clear out of the water.

If existence is reduced to just our bodies, then sex is merely a penetration of flesh. But the intercourse between two people

21

is more than just this merging. It begins well before that. Before touch. It begins as a thought. A ripple of air. The slight change in temperature, the minute trace of scent. The pull of some magnetic force. All that defies the illusion of separation. The idea that I began here, and he began there, and we were both confined to the lonely prisons of our bodies. Desire allowed us this escape, we began to touch before there was any contact between our skin. And in that boat, I felt him kiss me, the sea spray an extension of his wanting mouth, and I felt him hold me, the waves an extension of his body, but he never touched me with his hands, save that singular trespass of an inquisitive finger against the white beckoning of my naked wrist.

Ahmad's boat stopped in the middle of the water and the boys stared at us, bewildered by the erratic movements of that red boat in the sea. Ali waved us over, but the golden fisherman ignored him and kept going. The sky was overcast, but in that moment, the sun revealed herself from behind the gray clouds and illumined a path of gold in the water. He drove toward that path, to where it led to the sun, away from the shore, the witnesses, the flaming swords of *no* and *cannot*. What were the laws of man to stand in our way? What weight did those laws have in respect to the divinity of our desire? They felt flimsy, cardboard shams, when between us was an entire universe waiting to be conceived. But the punishments for our trespass were precisely designed to vanquish the flesh, to destroy the temple of our longing. Whippings, beatings, stonings. Punishments orchestrated to reduce the immensity of our desire back into the vulnerable smallness of our bodies, to leave it whimpering and contained within its bruised skin, resigned by fear to the cage of its broken ribs.

The whole of that time I sat silently with my eyes locked on his. But that golden path escaped us, and there was nowhere else for us to go, so he turned the boat and sped it with furious intention toward the shore, and we came upon that sand with such intensity that we all lurched forward when it stopped. Ahmad's boat was already there, and the boys waited on the sand, unhappily. Ali stood, furious. The girls scampered up. They knew there was something that was solely between that fisherman and me. He helped them out, one by one. I sat there, breathless, my scarf blown off my head, my hair tussled. Then, he extended his hand out to me.

There was such cataclysmic power in his touch. Explosions when our atoms met. Catastrophic in the magnitude of their impact. He held my hand and broke me open. We must have shone brilliantly on that shore, against the gray of the water and the sky. But there was no way to part by lingering. There were families on that beach. The village women, watching. Menacing police. The boys waiting on the sand. He held my hand for the duration of the time it took to help me stand on my feet, and step out of his boat. And in that time, eternity. In that time, a transcendence of this brief moment of mortality. Then, he let go and I walked away, without looking back. Because I couldn't look back. It would have been a telling. A confession. And all those other eyes already held the rage of accusation, the anger of having witnessed our shattering. So I walked away, and he must have turned to look out at the sea.

Storm clouds gathered. I took hold of Naghmeh's hand to ground me and a wind picked up off the water. Heavy, dark clouds rolled in. We loaded the cars quickly. Some of the girls drove with Javid and Pouya, the rest, including me, with Ali. Everyone in our car sat in silence as Ali drove, seething. A rain began. The farther we drove away, the harder it fell. Torrential. A heavenly vengeance.

ALI SLIPPED IN a Massive Attack CD. The car pounded with the bass. He had asked Bita to sit in the front seat beside him. He drove the curves of that mountainous road in the rain with unrelenting speed. Demoted to the backseat, my forehead pressed against the window and Naghmeh beside me, I tried to figure out what had just happened between that golden fisherman and me. Something of a certain immensity. Something that had shaken up the balance of things.

On one side of the narrow road yawned a deep gorge, at the far bottom of which a distant river meandered past jagged rocks. On the other side of the road, boulders of the mountain. Trucks drove into our lane to pass one another, barely pulling back into their own lane before near impact. Tunnels bored through the rocks, the fume of exhaust so heavy in them, a single cigarette thrown out the window would have ignited the air. Other cars blasted their horns through those tunnels, the sound blaring, as trucks drove recklessly past them and motorcycles raced between. The roads in Iran were notorious for their automobile fatalities. To drive them, even cautiously, was a brush with death. With dark humor, the truck drivers wrote, backwards, in large letters across the top of their windshields the name of the patron imam who was said to help those in moments of mortal danger, so that as they sped forward, the drivers of the cars in front could read *Ya Abolfalz* spelled out in their rearview mirrors.

When we reached the peak of the final mountain before descending to the city, the rain stopped abruptly, the sun returned and humidity set in. Bita rolled down her window. She chatted with Ali softly, consoling him until he slowed down, then rolled down his own window and placed his arm on the ledge. Bita laughed at his jokes, touched his arm on the steering wheel. The breeze through the open window blew back her headscarf, passed through the auburn locks of her hair. She stretched her arm out her window, fingers open in the wind, feeling beautiful in the attention of the man beside her. Our car pulsated with the music. Beguiled by the girl next to him, Ali failed to notice the black SUV two cars back in his rearview mirror, following our car. Not until it passed us, in the opposing lane, and a basiji police officer leaned out the window and motioned us to pull over, holding a rifle in hand.

It was as though a vacuum had sucked out the air of the car we sat in. As though the very breath had been sucked out of our lungs. A shared feeling of paralyzing terror gripped all of us, though theirs by experience and mine only in reaction to what I felt in them. Ali pulled over. Naghmeh tightened her headscarf, muttering, "Oh my G.d. Oh my G.d." Bita, drained of color, also readjusted her headscarf. Ali held tightly to the steering wheel and parked on the side of the road, then remembered the CD in the stereo. Too late to throw it out of

the window, he ejected it and slipped it, along with the other
CDs in the car, under his seat.

"Tell them you are my cousins. My mother's sisters' side,"
he said, quietly.

He turned off the car.

We sat in our car waiting for the Brothers to get out of
their car and approach us. I didn't know what to do, what to
expect. I had never felt so much fear. What did this mean?
What would happen to us now? Most of the young people I
had met in Tehran had had some run-in with the Basij, who
were different from the police. The sole job of the Basij was
to make sure everyone adhered to the tenets of Islam. They
were mythically cruel, obtuse, irrational. The kids told stories
about discovered parties, where the guests were beaten, taken
to dark prisons, held for days. Or on the streets, girls were
stopped, scrutinized for their hijab, assaulted, taken to dark
prisons, inspected for proof of their virginity, then abused
and held for days. Wine, dancing, the possession of unsanctioned books, films, music, any gathering of men and women,
all this was illegal, and the job of the Basij was to find those
who broke Islamic law, and arrest them, and punish them
without hearing, without due process, with impunity, with
righteous fury, in the name of their own god. And we had just
broken a handful of those laws. Female passengers in the company of a na-mahram male driver. Unsanctioned music. One
of us showing the locks of her unruly auburn hair, with her
bare arm stretched out of the window to catch the breeze.

I searched frantically through my satchel and found my
father's prayer tasbih. My father had never been a religious

man, but that tasbih belonged to an elderly uncle who, on his deathbed, had given the prayer beads to my father and blessed him. My father kept that tasbih in his desk, and after his own death, I took them. When I packed for this trip to Iran, I placed that tasbih beside my passport as a talisman.

I held those beads in my hand and prayed. The door to the black SUV opened after several minutes. The bearded driver, a tall, young man dressed in a black button-down shirt, black slacks, dark glasses, stepped out of the car, threw his spent cigarette to the dirt, stretched. The other bearded man, middle-aged and also dressed in black, got out of the car, too, still holding the rifle. They said something to each other, nonchalant, unhurried, in the theater of our windshield. The driver said something more, some final word, and the armed man laughed. Then they turned and walked toward us. They stopped before Ali's window, bent down, looked us over quietly. The unarmed Brother said to Ali, "Your identification card." Ali pulled out his wallet, took out his card, and handed it to the man. The man took it, put it in his breast pocket and said, "Now, follow my car down the mountain, to the station."

And that was that. We were going in. It might be days before my cousins and my uncle Behrooz would be able to locate where I was being held. Nobody allowed you a single phone call to inform your family, to tell them where you were or what had become of you. You disappeared until someone came to claim you, bribe money in hand.

"Please, G.d," I prayed. And just that. I couldn't find any other words, just, "Please, G.d," over and over and over. The Brothers returned to their car. Sauntered. Leaned against the door and lit cigarettes, looked at the mountains, took a few drags, then opened the door and got in.

Ali sat there, steering wheel still clutched in his hands. Bita was crying. Naghmeh, white, silent, held my hand in hers. Suddenly, Ali slammed the wheel with both his fists, and said, "No!" He opened his door, jumped out of the car and jogged up to the black SUV, his hands up in the air.

We watched him. He talked to the driver. Pointed in our direction. Gestured with his hands. We watched him. He kept talking. His movements became more natural. More animated. The Brother driving the car was now leaning in Ali's direction, resting his arm on the window. Then, that man laughed and turned to look in the direction of our car. Ali smiled, bowed his head, and the basiji extended his hand out the window, handing Ali his identification card back. Ali took the card, slipped it in his back pocket, placed his hand on his heart, bowed his head several more times, wove a jovial goodbye, and jogged back to our car.

He opened the door, got in and sat there, without a word. He waited until the black SUV pulled out into the road and drove away. Then, Ali started his own engine, allowed for several cars to pass before he pulled onto the road. We sat in silence for that whole duration, until Bita finally asked, "How?"

"I told them you were the daughters of my mother's sisters," Ali said. "That you were trusted to my care, and I had driven the three of you out for a day by the sea, and my head was pounding from listening to your nonsense for so long that I failed to notice Bita was sitting uncovered. I apologized and

28

told them how ashamed I felt for not being able to protect your honor, but they must understand how difficult a time I had been having, the constant vigilance needed to watch three girls for the duration of the drive to the seashore and back. I said I was exhausted by the responsibility of caring for you. When I said you had less intelligence than a bunch of chickens, they laughed. That's when he handed my ID back to me."

I HAD ARRIVED in Tehran's Mehrabad International Airport a few weeks earlier, in June of 2001. It was my first time returning to Iran since my family's escape. The last time I was in that airport, it had a different name, eighteen years back, when I was six years old. Then, my parents carried a single suitcase each. My mother had taken my hand firmly. She whispered something to my father before he separated from us. He got into the security checkpoint line for men. My mother walked with me to the checkpoint for women, where the Sisters stood behind folding tables. Women ahead of us had their luggage opened, gutted. The Sisters threw the contents onto the tables and the floor. They opened bottles, dug into the pockets of coats, tore linings. Some women were led into curtained rooms for further inspections. There were loud arguments. Crying. Whispered bribes. Women pled to be allowed to keep their rings, their necklaces. Everything of value was confiscated. The law was that you couldn't take any gold or currency out of the country. Guards stood nearby, young men holding big guns. My mother's turn came.

"Where are you going?"

"Europe. For vacation."

"When will you return?"

"Two weeks."

"Are you taking any jewelry or cash out of the country?"

"Nothing."

"What's in your suitcase?"

"Clothes. A pot or two for cooking, a hot plate."

"You need pots for cooking on vacation?"

"I cook my family's meals. I don't trust foreign food to be halal."

"Very good."

The Sister, in my recollection of that day in the airport, looks like any other Sister. Faceless. Draped in black cloth. Floating through the streets, in the parks, in the corridors of my primary school. They hid razors beneath their chadors, wiped lipstick off young girls by slashing their lips. They arrested women for wearing a color too close to the shade of lecherous intent. They looked for a lock of revealed hair, listened for a laugh too loud. They called over the Brothers in fatigues. Bearded, armed, the Brothers broke down the doors of homes. Tore through rooms with cyclonic fury, searching for bottles of wine, records and tapes, films, books, musical instruments. Weddings were hushed. Classrooms were monitored. Everything hidden.

My father stood in the line manned by the Brothers. We waited for him by the gate until we finally boarded the plane together. I don't remember much about the rest of that journey. We lived in various rooms in different European countries for a while. I remember nights where adults I didn't know sat around a table talking with my parents while I played quietly in a corner. They, like my parents, were waiting for their interviews at the American embassy. They shared notes, advice, stories about other refugees who had been denied visas and forced to return, and worse stories, still, about those who tried to cross borders in other ways. The interim between that last moment in Tehran's airport and the first time I arrived at Los Angeles International Airport is the hazy dreamscape of childhood. Loneliness. Uncertainty. An endless afternoon of looking out of an unfamiliar window at an unfamiliar street. Fear. But I remember clearly the last day I had been in this airport.

I got out of my seat and checked one more time to make sure my hijab was complete. My scarf tight and safety-pinned beneath my chin, my manteau buttoned. Then, I walked off the airplane, terrified that I had made some error in my dress. A man stood at the gate, holding a placard with my last name written in English. The rest of the passengers lined up for customs.

I had listened to the stories back in Los Angeles from the relatives and friends of my parents who decided to return to Iran to visit family or take care of their abandoned homes, properties, shuttered businesses, to find the photographs of their children, their ancestors, their heirlooms, to dig up the jewels of their deceased grandmothers, to inquire about bank accounts, lost friends, to tend to the grave of their dead fathers.

"The customs officials look for any reason to extract a bribe," they said.

"There is so much corruption," they said.

"It is better now than it was, they have relaxed a bit," they said.

"There is so much poverty, so much suffering."

"It is fine."

"It is dangerous."

"They've destroyed the country."

The customs officials were said to tear apart books. To hold up personal belongings to the light and criticize the traveler for indecency. Sometimes, people were identified, their names matched to family members on the Blacklist. Their passports were confiscated, and they found themselves imprisoned in Iran until the officials decided if and when they could leave. So when I found out that there existed an option to purchase a special pass that allowed travelers to skip the customs line for an expedited and more lenient search, I paid the surcharge.

The man with the placard greeted me with a bow of his head, took my carry-on from me and asked me to follow him. We walked down a long hallway to a door. He opened it, then stepped aside, implying that I should enter first. I walked in prepared for a dark cell, a single lightbulb dangling over a table, a few metal folding chairs. But instead, that door opened to an expansive room with high ceilings, outfitted like the receiving rooms of rich Iranians, all tufted antique French chairs and sparkling chandeliers and silk Tabriz rugs and gold-gilded coffee tables bearing crystals bowls brimming with fruits and nuts and marzipan. I could have been at an old aunt's luncheon in Beverly Hills. Save for the portraits of the dead Ayatollah on the walls. Oil paintings of him in ornate golden frames. Here, the Ayatollah smiling, his hand raised, blessing a crowd. There, the Ayatollah, serious, with a woman covered completely in a black chador in the background, a faceless entity, an unidentifiable presence, just a woman, any woman, in black hijab, perhaps the Ayatollah's wife. Portrait after portrait of the dead supreme leader's countenance, hanging from any wall you looked at.

The placard man told me to make myself comfortable, then asked, "Would you prefer cola, sherbet, or tea?"

I knew I had a role to play, that the costume of my hijab requested a specific female character. My understanding of this identity was a construction of contradictions. A composite of the way the West saw Iranian women, and the actuality of Iranian women. It borrowed from the front pages of newspapers and the covers of magazines the photographs of women in black hijab, crowds of them beneath bold headlines, caught with their mouths open, their fists raised in the air. It included stock characters in movies, the extras caricatured by Hollywood as fanatical, vicious, ignorant. Newsreels of a woman screaming in a language the viewer wouldn't understand. My idea of Iranian femininity incorporated the prejudices of my teachers and the parents of my American friends. And then, in stark contrast, there was the other part of that portrait pieced together from the actual women in my family and community, who were not fanatical, or vicious, or ignorant, who did not wave their fists or rage in tongues. It also took from their stories, about the way women in Iran were before the Islamic theocracy and the way women were forced to be after. Women who agreed to the hijab willingly, and everybody else.

And still another element. Aside from the Islamic laws mandated by the government, which most of the people I knew abominated, there were still the cultural expectations of proper female behavior. Modesty was the most obvious attribute of an upstanding Iranian girl, but there was a whole spectrum of what that modesty meant to each family. The Islamic State's interpretation was on the far right of that scale, my family's interpretation closer to the left. To my parents, hijab was a social travesty. But short shorts, midriff tops, and makeup belonged to the American girls. Sexual segregation in the public sphere was backwards. But boyfriends were strictly forbidden. So my construction of a feminine self was a bit Frankenstein. I had this idea of what I needed to be as a young woman in order to meet the gender expectations of my Iranian community in Los Angeles, but that idea was compounded by another identity, still. My American self, created outside the home and, perhaps, in protest of the parameters of self within that home, was only revealed when I was certain there were no witnesses who might report back to my family about whom I had been in the public sphere.

Now, standing in Mehrabad International Airport, returning to Iran by myself as a young woman after eighteen years of living in the United States as an immigrant, I needed to present a persuasive third self, the Iranian woman who seemingly accepted the State's dictates of female dress and decorum. The man with the placard asked me again what I would like to drink. I took my ramshackle idea of Iranian woman, pieced together from the news stories, and the personal stories, the soundbites, the lectures and all the other unspoken ways girls are told how to be, and I had to answer this man, now, about what I wanted to drink. My throat parched, my heart in my mouth, I replied, "A cup of water, please."

"Sparkling or flat?"

"Flat." In case sparkling suggested daring sophistication, or something.

He bowed his head and left to fetch the water. Another man entered the room wearing a dark suit, white shirt beneath, buttoned all the way up, no necktie. Because to wear a necktie in Iran meant that you aligned yourself with the West. So the authorities, the custodians of the republic, never wore them. But they did wear beards. Because beards indicated that you were conservative. This guy, with his buttoned shirt and dark suit and beard and tieless neck carried himself with an air of authority. I looked up at him, quivering, like a mouse cornered in the kitchen beneath the ominous shadow of a frying pan. He smiled down upon me and politely requested my passport. I reached into my backpack and gave it to him with a trembling hand. My Iranian passport. With a photo of me in it wearing a headscarf and a look of utmost piety. My American passport, and my American photo with my hair all wild and my eyes all wild and my lips glistening, lay hidden in the lining of my backpack. Because an American passport indicated disloyalty to Iran. I held out my Iranian passport and the tieless bearded man took it, smiled once more, then said he'd return as soon as they checked my records and located my luggage.

A family was escorted in. There were a whole lot of other gilded coffee tables and cushioned settees in that large room where the family could have sat, but the matriarch of the family came to the little section where I was, followed by her entourage of female relatives. They made themselves comfortable, asked the waiter for a round of tea, then greeted me. I responded in my best Farsi, with a shy hello. The matriarch asked what brought me to Iran.

It was the loss of my father that brought me here. Because I don't think I ever came to know him. He remained to me that mythical entity of childhood called *father*. He was strong. He had power. He could lift me up. He could terrify me with a look. He knew secrets about the world, the way things worked, like how to drive mountainous roads in the fog, how to find the ocean, how to whistle while riding a bike. I was utterly in love with him, in awe of him. Until he became sick. And grew weak. Until I heard him crying, secretly, in his room, and came to understand that he wasn't a mythical entity, but a man. He died before I had a chance to know that man. He remained a stranger to me. So I told her about my father and how I hoped to learn something of him here, in Iran. She told me they were returning from a shopping trip to Europe. Then, the matriarch began an onslaught of questions. Who I was, my age, where I grew up, my late father's full name, my mother's maiden name, where they grew up, what I studied and the level of my degree, if I worked, where I worked, did I have a fiancé?

I answered her questions as best as I could in my broken Farsi, without really asking myself why she took such interest in me. I answered her the way I imagined she wanted me to answer. When she asked if I came back to Iran searching for a husband, I told her that if an honest and good man came along, I was certainly not opposed to meeting him, but it wasn't something I sought. Then she asked if he had to be rich. I told her that purity of spirit was enough wealth in a man.

That's when it happened.

She leaned in, breathless, took both my hands in hers, looked deep into my eyes and said, "You must meet my eldest son. You are a perfect match for him."

I didn't see that coming. I knew the customs of khastegari. My mother and the other women in the family spoke of how they dated back in the old country, but I had never experienced it firsthand. I knew the stories, though. The mothers and grandmothers of young men searching high and low for eligible young women. The undercover exposés of reputations, not just of the young people involved in the relationship, but of their aunts, uncles, ancestors four generations back. Uncovering of genetic deficiencies or gambling addictions or debts or indiscretions, all before the formal introduction, the granting of permission, the chaperoned dates.

My mother had suitors. Formal ones. But she fell in love with my father, and their marriage was a rare one, a love match between a Jewish girl and a Muslim boy, the West Side Story of the Middle East. But relatives, particularly my mother's second cousin, had epic khastegari stories. This one aunt was so beautiful and so wealthy, suitors used to line up outside the door and wait their turn to sit with her in the parlor of their mansion in Tehran. Every day, lines of boys outside the door waited to be in her presence for a few minutes. And she'd come down the grand staircase, looking like a young Elizabeth Taylor, in the latest fashion from London, miniskirts and disco boots, Emilio Pucci dresses in silk or bell bottom jeans. She was the It Girl, and the boy she finally chose from the eager mass of suitors looked like he could have been one of the Beatles, handsome, with lamb chop sideburns, from an equally distinguished family of considerable wealth.

And here I was, not ten minutes back in Iran, where I had managed to stumble right into the rituals of an age-old tradition and a potential suitor. I was beside myself. It felt almost staged, too perfect a comedy. This woman, the matriarch of a traditional and upper-class family in Iran, deemed me suitable for her son? I had worried that my Americanness would seep out of me, that I wouldn't be able to present myself as a wholesome Iranian girl here, in Iran, where the most discerning would certainly see right through my act. The matriarch returned, followed by her son. If the initial interview was a comedy improvised by the universe, this boy was the punchline. I'm not a cruel person, but this kid, my age, couldn't have been better cast. Tall, ugly, awkward, lanky, collared shirt buttoned up and tucked into pressed jeans, and all nose. He walked in behind his mother, took one look at me, then sat down with such bored entitlement, you'd think he was the shah'n shah.

I had to turn my face and hold my breath and pinch my thigh very hard underneath my manteau to keep from laughing out loud. The matriarch read my behavior as a sign of my modesty, poor girl, so shy, she couldn't even look directly at her boy, which made me even more desirable of a candidate in her eyes. Meanwhile, she attempted to start a conversation between me and her prince, to which I could only respond in monosyllabic words, since I was choking on the tongue I kept biting to keep from laughing. Luckily, before I exploded, the waiter came back with a fresh pot of brewed tea, another pot of hot water, and glass teacups on a fine silver tray.

When I was a girl, whenever my parents had guests, my father would ask me to serve the tea. The serving of tea carried heavy social implications. It spoke volumes to those present about the type of girl I was. There was a whole ceremony to each step, from the way a glass was poured, to the level and the shade of the tea, to the arrangement on the tray, the way in which it was carried, to whom it was served first, the direction of the gaze and the correct intonation of the voice as it was offered. My father critiqued my etiquette after. If I carried out the presentation with mastery, he bestowed upon me the ultimate word of approval, that I had been a khanoom, a lady.

While my parents escaped Iran specifically so that their daughter could grow up free of the laws mandated by the Islamic theocracy to police women, they carried with them, from the old country, a clear sense of what a girl ought to be. She ought to be obedient. Modest in dress, in voice, in thought, in action. Intelligent, but not so much as to scare away a man. Soft spoken. She should dance well, with delicate wrist gestures and tosses of the hair and undulations of the hip. Play the piano. Blush at the applause of her parents' friends and relatives after the performance on the piano. She must be shy. Reserved. Dignified. And, of course, innocent of all things relating to sex. Until the night of her wedding, an

Iranian girl, and the adults responsible for her, protected her honor like vigilantes. That word, *honor*. A girl's honor meant a mind and a body untouched, unsullied by even the knowledge of sex. Lewd girls, a rather expansive category, not only shamed their families, but rarely managed to land themselves worthy husbands and marred the reputations of the other girls in that family. And it didn't matter that my parents were university-educated, or grew up in Tehran during the reign of the Shah, and went to discos and listened to rock and roll and drank and smoked and now railed at the barbaric treatment of women by the Islamic Regime. The idea of proper femininity sank its roots deep, deep into the psychic humus of the people, so that neither the love songs of the Beatles nor gyrations of Elvis's hips nor the dreamy-eyed American actors with their brazen brand of sexuality on the silver screen managed to really shift the limitations of Iranian female sexual expression. And when this generation of Iranians emigrated to the West, they packed this idea alongside their underwear, and brought it with them, and demanded, beyond all else, that the girls in the family continue to adhere to the old ways in their new country.

I used to leave the house with a change of clothes and lip gloss hidden in my backpack. I overachieved in school to hide my deviance. Sexual longings, whenever repressed, amplify and leave in their wake tremendous guilt. Because I broke a commandment, of the stone tablet variety, my identity was forged through the fire of that transgression, and I lived with a lot of guilt. When I left Los Angeles to return to Iran, it felt like climbing back up Mount Zion after the night of debauchery at the foothills. I thought I reeked of it. Yet that matriarch had held my hands and had come in real close, and she didn't notice the scent, but rather, identified me as a suitable marriage candidate for her son. And now, the waiter had brought in the tea, set it on the gilded coffee table, and here sat the matriarch, and here sat my future husband, and here I was, percolating with joy for this opportunity to play out such a fantastic scene.

A young woman's wooing of a potential suitor is not so much of the boy in question, as it is of the boy's mama. The matriarch reached for the teapot. I insisted on serving. She sat back. Eyes narrowed, waiting. The rest of the women waited, watched, calculated. I stood up, gracefully. I turned my face away from the boy. I poured that first glass with precision, from the pot of brewed tea, then diluted it with the pot of hot water until I reached the right shade of amber, the right level in the cup, and I held that tea glass out to the matriarch with doe-like humility. Then, I served the other waiting women, in order of age, the eldest first. Finally, I poured the boy a glass of tea. I extended it to him, looking down at the floor like a demure maiden. He took it from me. I paused a moment before retracting my hand. Then I held out the silver bowl of rock sugar with a slight glance in his direction, waiting for him to select one to put in his mouth or drop in his tea, whatever way he liked it. After he took a piece of rock sugar, I took one, too, just a small piece, not too much. I looked up at him and put that piece of sugar in my mouth to suck. Slowly.

Such innuendos, such subtleties of courtship are necessary in a highly sexually repressive state. This seduction of her son, acted out without the slightest hint of immodesty, just floored the mama of my future husband. Such a wholesome girl, so shy, so reserved, so respectful, and so well versed in the customs, despite being raised in the United States? And on top of all that, the visa to America that came with the package!

"All that is left," she said, "is to request your uncle's permission."

In the meantime, I had forgotten completely about the tieless bearded guy who held my passport. Until he cleared his throat behind me, apologized for interrupting our dialogue, handed my passport back with a smile, and said that my luggage awaited me downstairs in baggage claim.

That was it? The inquisition I had prepared for came from a rather unlikely source for a rather unexpected reason. Didn't this man want to know about my religious background? Or my political ideologies? Or my familial connection to several names on the Blacklist? Or my disloyalty to my country of birth, and why I chose to become a citizen of America? He smiled. He handed me my passport. He told me where to find my luggage and mentioned that it remained untouched. Then, bearded, tieless man, custodian of the regime, said, rather sincerely, "Welcome back. I hope you find what you have come seeking." He bowed, humbly, and left.

I turned to find the matriarch beaming, and the boy slouched in his chair, a bit of spittle on the corner of his lip, with a bit more interest in me, now that he knew I liked to suck my rock sugar. "Well, let's go and find your uncle," the matriarch said.

We took the escalator down from the lounge. And there stood Behrooz. A giant of a man. Tall, with mirth in his eyes, straight of back and proud and so happy to see me. I ran to him, into his open arms, into the safety of his embrace.

"Everything went well?" he asked.

"I have a little problem," I said.

He noticed the matriarch standing behind me, and behind her, the entourage of women and the nose boy. She took no time to introduce herself, list my merits, congratulate him on our reunion, praise him on what a gem of a girl I appeared to be. "My son and your niece have taken an interest in one another. Would you be open to the two of them seeing each other?"

And Behrooz said, "Certainly. I'll give you my phone number."

The blood drained from my face. Cold sweat. Maybe this wasn't some universal jest, played out for my entertainment. Maybe this was how young, unsuspecting girls were forced into marriages by well-meaning relatives. My uncle wrote down his phone number for her, along with the family name. She then turned to me and bade me farewell until, of course, my first date with her son, where she, too, would be in attendance, along with a couple of aunts and maybe an elderly grandmother. After a rather forward kiss on both my cheeks, she walked off to where servants and a chauffeur waited for her and her family, leaving me bewildered in her wake.

Just then, a group of girls walked by. They wore their headscarves loosely, revealing their hair. They had red painted lips, wore high heels, tight jeans and tailored manteaus that hugged their curves. They looked like models. They stood nearby, and one took out a pack of cigarettes and offered it to her friends. They turned to a stationed guard and asked him for a light. He smiled obligingly and lit their cigarettes. The girls thanked him, turned to one another, talking out loud. They openly looked at the single men who walked by, whispered their assessments, and laughed.

"You haven't been in Iran an hour and you managed to snag the most eligible bachelor in Tehran?" Behrooz said. I turned to look at him. I didn't know how long I had been staring at those girls. Behrooz put his hand on my shoulder and said, "Did you know that family has a monopoly on the manufacturing of screws and nails in all of Iran?" He took hold of my luggage and started walking toward the exit. "All those buildings out there, held together by that family alone. Your suitor is the heir of a tremendous fortune. Congratulations. You'll be very well taken care of."

I couldn't walk. I couldn't trust the earth beneath my feet. The laws I had expected to govern the universe here didn't seem to apply. Where were the angry Sisters? Why had that bearded, tieless Brother spoken kindly to me? Why didn't this stationed guard harass these girls for indecency? And if not for the restrictions imposed by the State, weren't these girls worried that somebody who knew one of them might see them and make them the subject of rumors and gossip that would inevitably lead to the shame of their whole family? I noticed Behrooz still watching me, with concern now.

"I don't think that boy is right for me," I said to him.

"Of course not." He laughed and patted me on the back. "I was joking. When your future mother-in-law calls, I'll just mention that we are Jewish and that will bring an abrupt end to this love story."

It was June, and the heat came in gusts through the automatic doors each time they slid open to where taxi cabs honked, while people loaded and unloaded suitcases and embraced madly, or wept, or stood vacant-eyed, waving goodbye.

"I don't recognize anything here," I said.

I didn't know how to step forward, how to enter the world that waited outside that exit. How to be. Who to be. My last memory of the country beyond those automatic doors was the morning of our escape. I lay in the backseat of my parents' car on our way to this airport. I looked up at the stretch of sky, interrupted by the passing buildings and telephone lines, and I understood that I was losing something. I tried to memorize the shade of blue, the gold outline of the gray concrete high-rises as the sun rose behind them, reflected in the glass of their windows. Beyond that last memory, I knew nothing about this place, this vatan that both belonged and did not belong to me. I spoke the language in fragments. I knew the culture in pieces. The narrative of Iran was a disjointed story for me, told by a hundred contending voices, each claiming authority. And here I stood, a young woman, returned . . . home?

Behrooz held out his hand. "Don't be afraid," he said. "Just observe, quietly, for a while. Soon, you'll come to know it as your own." I nodded, took his hand and we walked toward that exit, the doors that opened and shut, opened and shut.

.   .   .

WHEN I ARRIVED at Behrooz's apartment, his wife and his sons, Javid and Pouya, were there to greet me. My uncle sat me down at the kitchen table and told me that there were nuances to public behavior in Iran that I did not understand, an entire language of social decorum, taboos, restrictions that required experience to learn and navigate. The margin for errors was small. "I want you to stick with either Javid or Pouya when you leave the house. For a little while. They will keep you safe until you learn your way."

Then, Pouya asked, "Do you want to come with me to a pool party?"

Jet-lagged and disoriented, dressed in a hijab that was ghastly in comparison with the sleek interpretations of hijab I saw on our drive home from the airport, I went with my cousin to a beautiful brick home in a neighborhood of other beautiful, large brick homes and old trees. In a drawing room full of antiques and heavy drapery and fine furniture, girls in bikinis lounged on the couches sipping drinks and eating olives. I took off my hijab and hung it on the coat rack by the door, which was already heavy with manteaus and headscarves. Pouya and I walked into a lush backyard surrounded by high walls, and there, diving into a blue swimming pool surrounded by girls in bikinis and designer sunglasses, was Ali.

He swam the length of the pool and pulled himself out, water streaming from his auburn curls, down his muscled torso. He had a compact, powerful body. Eyes the shade of honey. A fierce hunger in them. A strong chin. He took a quick glance at me, slapped Pouya's back with his wet hand in greeting, then turned back and asked, "You want to see a crocodile?"

The girls around the pool responded with a unanimous yes. He got down onto the ground at my feet, balancing himself on his hands and his toes as though ready to do push-ups, then he slithered and curved his way back to the pool's edge, and flopped in sideways, impressively crocodile-esque. The girls squealed with delight. He swam the length of the pool and with perfect fluidity, got out, jumped into the air, flipped, and dove back in.

Ali had been Pouya's best friend since boyhood. This was his parents' house, but his father had died six months earlier, and though he was the youngest child of six, last in a line that included five daughters, the house now belonged to him. He also owned a villa in the northern Caspian Sea region of Iran. Ali was the playboy of the Tehran scene. Not a girl poolside he hadn't discreetly had already.

"So you're Pouya's cousin from Los Angeles?" he asked me.

I felt the tension of the other girls, the quiet appraisal of my sexual appeal, the calculations of whether I presented a threat or not in their contest for this man's attentions. But Ali was Pouya's best friend, a brother to him. And I knew the codes of this culture well enough to know that if a man had a friend who was like a brother to him, he kept his hands off his friend's female kin, his sisters, his cousins, any blood relation of his unless the man's intentions were marriage. And if that was the case, he'd ask permission from his friend before he began the courtship, and he wouldn't touch the girl until she was given to him for keeps. So when I told Ali my name, and he invited me to swim, and I declined and told him I was there to only watch, he returned to his performance, but this time for my sake, which he knew, and the girls knew, and I understood. But I had just ended an obsessive and all-consuming love affair before arriving in Tehran. I had left Justin behind in Los Angeles. In truth, I had escaped Los Angeles to leave Justin behind. So I ignored Ali.

The girls surrounded me, wanting to know who I was, where I came from, how it was in LA. I wanted them to like me. I was tired from my journey. The sun felt good on my skin. The walls were high enough to keep the music and the sound of our laughter from reaching the street and alerting the police to our illegal gathering. The colors of that afternoon appear hazy in my memory, like a faded Polaroid. Muted sunlight, a faint blue pool, the slowly erased familiarity of a handsome man's face. On the borders of that image are the partially nude bodies of young women, their gaze hidden behind sunglasses. It could have been a scene in any Los Angeles backyard. And so, in a state of half dream, I forgot where I was, and I allowed myself to be.

AT LAX, MY mother had held me in her embrace for a long time. I finally pulled away from her, assured her that I'd be fine and turned to walk to my gate. I had on my Das Meindl boots, my trekking backpack on my back, my cash and American passport hidden in its lining, my suitcase checked. A couple weeks ago, I had quit my job at a subtitling firm in Hollywood. That same night, Justin and I sat in my parked car on Cahuenga and Hollywood Boulevard. Outside, the steady current of people walked by, weirdos and junkies and club goers and tourists dazzled by the grime-covered stars beneath their feet.

"I don't know when I'll return," I told him.

Justin looked straight ahead. He didn't show any emotion, but I could see his fury in the tightness of his jaw. His hurt in the straight line of his lips. A helicopter with search lights passed overhead. In the distance, sirens wailed endlessly. I imagined whomever they were hunting and what it might feel like to be hunted. Running through the crowded streets. Cold. Afraid. Dodging the lights of the marquees. The flashing advertisements. The costumed characters, Mickey Mouse and Marilyn Monroe, the man painted silver, the handful of Michael Jacksons moonwalking, the guy holding the sign about the Second Coming, screaming above the noise and the traffic, "Repent! Repent!"

It had been four years since my father's death, and I felt like I was suffocating. I waited in that car, carefully reading the man who sat silently beside me. "You never loved me," Justin said, finally. He got out of my car, slammed the door. I called him, again and again, but he didn't pick up his phone. I left messages apologizing, explaining, pleading for forgiveness.

I had met Justin five years earlier in the parking lot of a strip mall in the San Fernando Valley, at the beginning of the summer, so that the heat was already the intolerable hell-furnace the Valley is known for, and the air heavy with that brown death that lingers just above your head, and the sea-gulls suspended in the sky as that strange haze rose from the asphalt and made everything seem like a desert mirage. He walked toward me from that warped light rising from the parking lot, shirtless, long hair loose about him, green eyes, smooth skin, an apparition of beauty. He stood before me, then said hello in a baritone I felt in a part of me strangers don't often touch.

At home, my father was dying, slowly. From Lou Gehrig's disease. A darkness entered our house. I used to punch the walls in my bedroom with my bare fists after spoon-feeding pureed baby food to my father, while my mother used a machine to suction out what he couldn't swallow. I needed desperately to pull my life apart from that death. Justin's arms, the weight of him, the urgency of his desire in contrast to that other urgency, offered me an escape. When I was with Justin, it felt like the gulps of air a drowning man takes each time he struggles to the surface to breathe.

And it wasn't just that, either, the escape of death through desire. I grew up choked by restrictions. My parents had left behind a whole world they understood in Tehran, and settled in the staggering isolation of a Los Angeles suburb. They barely spoke the language. They couldn't grasp the culture. Everything felt foreign and dangerous. They learned about the America outside our door from the TV in our living room, through the nightly news and sitcoms. The news promised kidnappings and rape and gang violence. The sitcoms showed broken families, unruly teenagers, dysfunction. The world outside the home was hostile to our ways. Violent. Unwelcoming. My parents needed to protect me from the lawlessness, the waywardness of America. I was to walk straight home after school. I was to keep my mind on my studies. If I met friends at the movies, I was dropped off right before the film began and picked up immediately after. I wasn't allowed to sleepover at anyone's house, and school dances were a leniency only because teachers were in attendance. Parties were out of the question.

Everything with Justin was a trespass. I used to go hiking with him in the coastal mountains where we wandered off the trails to hidden crevices in the valleys of those mountains. We spent the afternoons lying on warm slabs of granite by the creek. We climbed the side of those mountains to overlooks. Once, we walked into a den of rattlesnakes. Once, a cloud of bees swarmed over our heads. We used to crawl through the hole in the chain-link fence to cross the ledge of the dam, past the "No Trespassing" signs, to swim in the lake. At night, we drove to secret parties in old, abandoned factories where DJs played electronic music until the sun came up. Then, we'd stumble out, drive to the drum circle at Venice Beach, or go to Lenny's house. Lenny was an old black man, a friend of Justin's father. He had known Justin since Justin was an infant. Lenny lived in an apartment full of old records and so many potted plants, the air inside his home felt tropical. He would pour a glass of wine, roll a joint, and put on a record, blues, jazz, funk, and talk about the music. I spent whole mornings with him in the study of Funkadelic's "Maggot Brain" or War's "Get Down."

Sometimes, Justin's father showed up, too. Justin was the child of this black man and a white woman, the result of a momentary love. Justin's father talked about another America, one I didn't know existed, having grown up sheltered in an upper-middle-class white suburban neighborhood, where I was both poor and the only dark-haired, dark-skinned child at school, where the history textbooks glossed over the Middle Passage and had illustrations that depicted smiling *Indians* engaged in the tallow industry of the pueblos beneath the loving guidance of the halo-headed padres. Justin's father's stories of brutality and corruption, not just historical but current, sounded familiar. He spoke of a system of governance and policing that seemed as menacing as the country my family had escaped decades ago. My parents were too caught up with my father's illness to know where I was and what I was doing. I told them I was at school or the library. That I was studying. Researching. And I was, indeed, learning.

Then my father died.

In that moment of shattering, I understood the prison I'd made for myself within Justin. Though he had pulled me out of the prohibitions of my parents' fears, he paroled that freedom. I was his girl. His, only. When we walked together, if another man looked at me, Justin would seethe with jealousy. He would accuse me of walking in a way that attracted attention, of being inviting. After a while, I learned to keep my eyes down in the streets, to keep my mouth in a hard, thin line for fear that Justin might see me smiling and accuse me of looking at another man, then fly into a fit of rage. I felt smaller and smaller. Anxious. Encaged. I couldn't breathe. I needed to escape.

It took a while for me to realize where to go so that Justin wouldn't follow me. He had followed me when I left to study at the university in Berkeley. Followed me when I returned to LA to work as an elementary school teacher at a yeshiva in Hollywood. After a year at the yeshiva, I got a job at a subtitling firm in the high-rise next to the CNN building, and I sat, day in and day out, behind a computer screen at a window overlooking the hills and the Hollywood sign, overseeing the subtitling of films distributed to twenty-five European countries. It was drudgery. Meaningless, futile work. And Justin was more and more demanding that I remain a small satellite in the orbit of his needs.

Then, a few years after my father's death, Uncle Behrooz was granted a visa to visit America. In the evenings, we'd gather at my grandmother's house and he would tell stories about his adventures in Iran. He went trekking often through the wilderness and had friends among the nomads and the shepherds. He was welcomed in remote, unknown villages as an honored guest. His stories were so vivid, so full of life, of magic. The Iran of Behrooz's stories was not the Iran of the evening news, or the Iran of my parents' memories. It did not carry the same threat, or the sad nostalgia. It felt like a place bigger than life, full of possibilities and experiences I thought could only exist in books. I sat and listened to my uncle, captivated. He looked at me, and somehow understood that I was searching for something. "Come to Iran," he invited me. "I will take you with me on these journeys, to experience them for yourself."

And I knew, then, what I had to do to be free.

I fought with my mother about going back. She pleaded, threatened, tried to reason me out of it. She and my father had risked their lives to bring me to America. They had sacrificed everything so that their daughter could grow up with freedom, and go to school and go to college and have a career and buy a home in a nice neighborhood. But I felt trapped, by the sorrow of my father's death, by the crippling memories of his suffering. I'd sit in traffic on the way to work, clutching the steering wheel, and think about my job, my school loans, and credit card debts. I'd think about Justin, and the marquees and the advertisements. I walked on those grime-covered stars on the sidewalk and thought about all the absurdities. Life couldn't be just this. I argued until my mother saw she couldn't win. I bought my ticket, packed my trekking stuff into my backpack, and a suitcase of other things, and she dropped me off at LAX, held me tight in her embrace, until I pulled away from her and got on the plane.

I carried a secret with me, on board. A ticking time bomb, strapped to my chest. Since adolescence, I'd had a heart issue. My heart would start racing, 240 beats a minute. I had gone to doctors, and they had wired me up to all sorts of machines, and they never seemed to find the cause. When I told my mother I was going to Iran to live with her brother Behrooz for a while and trek the mountains, she finally gave in with one caveat, that I go and have a full check-up on my heart, to make sure everything was in order. I went to a cardiologist, had an EKG, ran on a treadmill, did an echocardiogram, and while they couldn't catch the arrhythmia, they discovered two holes in my heart. An atrial septal defect, which had been there, unnoticed, since birth. To keep me alive, my heart had to do a lot more work than a normal, healthy heart. This strain had enlarged my right atrium to the point where I was due for cardiac arrest. I needed open heart surgery, stat.

I didn't have time for surgery. I wasn't ready to face my own mortality. My bags were packed. I needed to leave. I decided not to tell anyone about my malformed heart until I returned. Once I came back, I'd deal with the whole heart thing. I got on that airplane with my broken heart, my father gone, and Justin behind me. There would be open skies for a while. Then the layover in Heathrow. Then, finally, Iran. And there, I would find something. To fill the holes. To heal them.

MY SECOND DAY in Tehran, a garden gate burst open in front of me on my solitary walk to the neighborhood produce bazaar. Out ran a dazzling rooster, flashing emerald green and brick red, followed by two children who were, in turn, followed by a white-haired old man in sandals, all of whom were laughing in their chase of the feathered escapee, who ran around and around a tree, then down the street with his captors in fierce pursuit.

This filled a hole in my heart. Just this. The unexpectedness of it. The joy of it. The colors of the rooster, emerald green that turned to purple that shone black in the shift of light, the sound of the children's laughter, the protests of the rooster, the half-hearted curses of the old man. In that moment, I lost myself. I lost the boundaries between me and the world before me. I became the chase, the laughter, the freedom. When I returned to myself, again, I was on an unfamiliar street, the signs of which were written in an alphabet I could barely read, with cars that ignored the traffic signals and the pedestrians.

The day I buried my father, something changed. It is a difficult thing to write about, even still, because it transcended words. Something broke open, sent my consciousness free-wheeling beyond everything I thought I understood. I knew, instantly, that the body was an illusion, that time was an illusion, that suffering was an illusion. That the separation between me and plum and tree and sunlight did not exist. I felt as though I had awoken from a deep sleep. It was the first of May when he died. All the leaves on the trees were new, and they glistened in the sun, and each time the wind blew through them, they sang. Suddenly, the whole of the universe was singing. Or it had been, all along, but now, I could hear it. I lost myself for hours like that, to the symphony of wind and leaves. People passed me in the streets, and I felt as though they had walked right through me, the impact of their humanity like a punch in the gut. I couldn't separate myself from the overwhelming, aching beauty of the world that surrounded me. I kept losing the boundary between where I ended and the universe began. Once, sitting in a café, I watched the men and women in gray suits walking to work, briefcases in hand, worried, distracted, a steady stream of them coming and going in and out of buildings, and then I saw an old woman walking slowly among them. She stopped and looked to the pavement. It was autumn. Scattered leaves. She stooped over carefully. The men and women kept going. She bent down and picked up something orange. It was a butterfly. A monarch. She stood illuminated among those gray people and held life cupped in her hands, fluttering, broken. I watched her through the glass and couldn't stop weeping.

It happened often, after my father's death, that I'd lose myself to this awe. When I moved out of my parents' home to study in Berkeley, Justin and I used to drive all over Northern California in his beat-up old car, before all the roads and highways became mapped by satellites, when it was still possible to explore. We packed cheese and bread, he had his camera and I had my poetry notebook, we got into that car and just drove. Nowhere. Searching. One early morning we came to a green pasture. Cows on the dew-soaked field, one laboring, about to birth. Then suddenly, out slipped a calf, wet, encased in a film, into the soft, overgrown grass, and from that grass, in that very instant, flew out a whole cloud of startled blackbirds. We drove for hours seeking these treasures. And when we stood witness to them, they weakened my knees, shortened my breath, and each time, brought me to weep.

Over time, I saw the grace of the universe and it still pierced my heart, but I kept going. I had term papers to write, books to read. A job to work. People to meet. Arguments to fight, bills to pay, friends to lose and keep. Life pulled me back into herself, and I learned to ignore the moments of devastating beauty so I could keep on going. It wasn't possible to be awake like that, and live. But once in a while, it happened that I'd be walking in the streets, and suddenly, I'd feel myself rising, above me, above the whole city, and I could see us, all of us, in the apartments and in the stores and in the classrooms, in courtrooms and banks and streets, each of us trapped by the lonely illusion of our own being, until moments of rapture and tragedy broke us open and allowed us transcendence. Sometimes I stopped for it, for the feeling to pass. Sometimes, I ignored it and kept going.

But now I was in Iran. And among the many reasons I was standing where I was standing, on a street with signs in a language I could barely read, was that I felt incomplete. There were the glimpses of something beyond the ego whenever I experienced those moments of rapture, but that didn't answer the question posed by my family, my professors, my employers, friends, acquaintances, strangers in the street about who I was meant to be. I was twenty-four now, a college graduate, and I had already bounced from an aborted start in a career in teaching to an aborted start in a career in the film industry, and when people asked who I was, I couldn't very well answer them with *I am the stardust of the universe*, or *I am everything that has and has not been*. People wanted specifics. It meant compiling the list of attributes, test scores and transcripts, accomplishments, degrees, debts, economic class, future potential, career path, tastes, the contents of my wardrobe, my politics, the way I spoke, the music I listened to, the color of my skin, the books on my shelf, the style of my worship, the size of my shoe, and clearly stating the summation of all that into the logarithm of a concise identity.

I left Iran as a child and arrived in America when I was almost seven. My identity was still in formation, still green, but I had a sense of the rules governing who I should be. But then, suddenly, I was plucked out of the society where those rules applied and dropped into a whole new one. Tehran to

Los Angeles. And those rules didn't apply anymore. Even the words my parents had taught me sounded like gibberish in LA. I had to discard my identity or hide it, either in shame or to protect myself from the taunts and the jeers about my clothes, my manners, the foods I ate, my inability to pronounce "th." I had to find, quickly, quickly, a new identity, and since now I had lost all faith in identities, in general, I pulled together a sham of a mask and hoped that it was enough to ward off the jackals.

It never fit. Not the new one I tried on, and not the old one I tore off. So I was left always feeling naked. And naked is vulnerable. I thought that here, in Iran, I might find something of myself, some missing piece left behind that, once found, would complete me. And that rooster, those children and their grandfather . . . that was not a thing of Los Angeles. Inconsequential as it was, it was still a story that belonged to these streets and, perhaps, it belonged to me now, too. So I took it, thinking that if I gathered enough stories, if I lived enough moments within Iran, I might be able to stitch it into a wholeness, wrap it about myself and say, "This, this is who I am."

I found the bazaar that sold fruits and vegetables. Wooden crates full of tomatoes. Trays piled high with purple egg plants. Mountains of apricots. Rusted scales with weights. Men who shouted out the prices of their produce. I stood there amidst the noisy colors of it, uncertain of what to do. Bell peppers. I had to buy bell peppers for my uncle's wife. I found a produce merchant who sold them. A handwritten sign displayed the price per kilo. I selected a few, which he weighed on his scale and placed in a bag. My first task accomplished, I turned to walk back to the apartment when an old man with a wheelbarrow started to follow me.

"Miss," he said. "Allow me to carry your bag."

"No, thank you. It is light enough."

"Please?" He had on dusty brown pants, patched, held by a belt of rope. A woolen cap on his head. His hands gnarled, the skin of his face weathered, eyes cloudy. "Please?"

I placed my single plastic bag in the wheelbarrow. "I'm going in that direction," I motioned. We walked in silence. I watched him from the corner of my eyes, his trudging gait, his shirt too big, his threadbare vest, his body gaunt, his mouth toothless, lips sunken in. "Why are you working still, father?"

"My wife is back in Afghanistan. She is sick. All our children are lost."

He looked so tired, and I could feel it coming, again, the surge of it, welling up inside me. Not now, I told myself, not here, not in these unfamiliar streets. It was a battle. An existential war. How could I not see him? How could I not allow his fatigue to fill me up, to slow down my own feet? We came to the apartment gate.

"Here?" he asked.

I didn't know what else to do, so I took out all the cash in my satchel, put it in his wheelbarrow, grabbed my bag, and turned away as fast as I could, rang the intercom, ran up the stairs and into the apartment where I told my uncle's wife what had happened.

"Well, go down and tell him to wait," she said. "I'll pack him some food."

That afternoon, when my cousin Javid came home from work and heard the story of my first experience in the marketplace, he offered to take me shopping. "How about I take you to a nice store where you can buy a more fashionable manteau?" he said. "What you are wearing is a little outdated."

Javid and I drove to a part of Tehran that had boutiques in white stone buildings, stylish mannequins in storefront windows, and young women with shopping bags and expensive purses sitting at outdoor cafés, sipping iced coffee drinks, smiling at young men in designer jeans and sneakers. Here, I was safe. Here, I was too concerned by my baggy, shapeless hijab to lose myself. Here, the song of the universe was drowned out by the bugle and horns of the ego. Everybody was so pretty. Everything so shiny. I bought a few linen manteaus, finely tailored. I bought a silk headscarf in saffron red, another in cream. I bought almond oil from an apothecary shop where the salesman promised it would bring out the sheen of my hair. Javid and I sat at one of the outdoor cafés and sipped coffee glacés.

On our way back to the car, we passed an old woman sitting on the sidewalk. She had an embroidered sheet folded before her, and on it were spread bundles of herbs tied with twine. Javid hurried his pace.

"Daughter?" she said.

I stopped.

"I grew these in my garden," she said.

I knelt down to look at her herbs. She smiled at me.

"Where are you from, child?" she asked. I looked into her eyes. Her eyes smiled, too.

"America," I said. Her smile was so deep, I found myself drowning, again. I looked away from her, pretended to select from the bundles.

"You carry a sadness in your heart," she said.

"We'll take the basil," Javid said. He picked up a bouquet of opal basil and paid her.

"I will pray for you, daughter," she said.

"You reveal too much of yourself," Javid said on the way to the car. "It attracts attention. You can't be that open here."

The car smelled strongly of basil, the perfume of it a silent reminder of an old woman's garden, of seeds sown in the hard earth, of hope, of seedlings crowning through dark soil, reaching for the light.

ON THE THIRD day of my homecoming, I found myself before a police chief, who sat behind an enormous desk of some dark colored wood, cherry or mahogany, in a green leather swivel chair. The office was stifling. Behind the police chief, nailed to the wood paneled wall, hung an oil painting of Ayatollah Khomeini with his signature smile and a pink tint to his cheeks. I saw his image everywhere, on billboards, posters in banks, murals on the sides of buildings. I supposed the artist of this particular painting meant the portrait to look something like the image of a benevolent father, but I noticed a leer in the Ayatollah's eyes that didn't befit the role. Who knows? Maybe the artist meant for the eyes to leer. Maybe the pink cheeks and the terrifying eyes were an intentional, albeit hidden, message by the artist, who created the noble portraiture as requested by the Orwellian state, but included, nonetheless, his own meaning.

"Do you know why you are in my office?" the police chief asked me, again.

I looked away from the portrait of the Ayatollah to the police chief. Bald. Shiny. Small eyes. Trim little mustache. I looked down quickly to my own hands clasped in my lap. This moment afforded no room for error, because the wrong look, the wrong tone, could escalate this little offense, my shameless ankles, to dangerous proportions. I shook my head no.

"Do you understand Farsi?" the police chief asked me. It was hot, he was sweating, and I could smell him in the stagnant air. His eyes bored into me.

"A little," I responded in Farsi, with an intentionally exaggerated American accent.

"You are here because of your indecency," the police chief said, then looked at me silently for a long, long while, with his forehead wrinkled, his chin tucked down, waiting for the accusation to sink in. I kept my eyes down, my head lowered. "This is a public space created so the youth can have a place to exercise their bodies," he said. "And your appearance causes an unhealthy distraction. It ruins the wholesomeness of their endeavors to achieve a healthy body through a healthy mind."

To escape his interrogation within that suffocating office, I thought back to an evening, less than a week earlier, when I lay partially naked in the grass of a backyard in Encino Hills amidst a group of sprawling, nude strangers. I had told my yoga teacher I was heading to Iran for an indeterminable while to find answers to some indeterminable question, and she said, "Come with me to this sweat hut ceremony. It'll give you clarity."

I had driven to San Fernando Valley, up some street that needed paving, through a cluster of dusty eucalyptus, onto the driveway of a secluded home. I rang the doorbell, and there she stood, the shaman. She led me to a backyard, where a bunch of people I didn't know were contorted into various yoga positions, completely naked. I was the youngest among them. "You don't have to get naked," the shaman said. "But that's how it's done."

"The immodesty of your appearance is an affront to our intentions," the police chief said. The harshness in his voice pulled me back from Encino Hills to that hard chair in the cloistered office, before the enormous wooden desk. I played with a button on my manteau. I was wearing one of the new linen ones I had purchased with Javid, along with my saffron-colored headscarf and a long white skirt, loose enough to hide my curves. I had on tennis shoes. The offense? I hadn't worn socks. Only a bit of skin was visible between the hem of my skirt and my shoes, just a fraction of ankle. It was hot and, beneath all that hijab, I was sweating something dirty, so I figured I'd allow my poor feet some respite. And the tennis shoes did look better without socks. Ali had called Pouya that morning and invited both of us for a game of tennis at a sprawling park devoted to athletic pursuits. Soccer fields, tennis, rugby, basketball courts. It was the first time I stepped out onto city streets not looking like some village girl from a religiously conservative family. When we arrived at the park, I got out of Pouya's car, walked with the boys in the direction of the tennis courts and, just then, out of nowhere, the Sisters of Islam, a whole gang of them in their black chadors, formed a tight circle around me, scowling, furious, shrill with indignation.

"How can you leave the house looking like this?" they asked me.

"How are you related to these two boys?"

"Is it for them that you are so shamelessly revealing your body?"

This wasn't the first time I found myself surrounded by the Sisters. When I was four years old, my mother took me to my first dentist visit. She promised that if I was good, afterwards she'd take me to Shahr e Bazi to ride the Ferris wheel and eat cotton candy. I was good, and she kept her promise. It was dusk when we left the dentist's office and arrived at the park entrance. The lights of the Ferris wheel twinkled and, next to that, the cotton candy machine spun. It was the early days of the Ayatollah's rise to power. The hijab, the Islamic State dictated by sharia, all that was still new. People didn't really understand what was happening yet. The women were told that they had to leave the house in full hijab, but until very recently, they had been leaving the house in whatever they pleased.

My mother was a young woman taking her daughter to the dentist and the park. She wore a loose-fitting sweater, a belt at her waist, and a scarf thrown over her hair as a nod to the new rules. But the Islamic regime meant business, and my mother's fashionable interpretation of Islamic law was not appreciated, certainly not by the black chador-clad Sisters.

Just as we entered that park, they surrounded her. They circled tight around us, pushed her, asked her how she could look like such a whore in public, yelled at her. To appease them, she removed her belt so that the sweater was formless. This didn't satisfy the Sisters. They called over a Brother. A young man, from some far-flung village, outfitted in the garb of authority. He carried a gun. He lectured my mother about her appearance. I tried to pull her out of their circle, toward the light of the Ferris wheel. I tugged at her hand, I whined, I cried. Finally, they let her go. They told her to leave the park at once and never enter the public sphere dressed so shamelessly again. My mother picked me up and rushed to hail a cab. I watched that Ferris wheel grow farther and farther into the distance from the backseat window.

And now, back after nearly two decades, I stood again in the circle of the Sisters, without my mother, trying to defend myself against their accusations. The more I spoke, the louder they yelled, until Ali stepped in and apologized to them, then sat down on the hot asphalt at the hem of their chadors, took off his own sneakers, took off his sweat socks, jumped up, handed them to me and ordered me to go to the car and put his socks on. Barked the order. Because he understood that this was what the Sisters wanted to hear. This was what they wanted to see. My subjugation and shame. I recognized Ali's gallant move, but a fire raged through me. I turned, walked to the car, put his damp sweat socks on and walked back, visibly angry. I looked ridiculous. I felt humiliated. I stood before the Sisters and asked, perhaps with the wrong tone, if this would do. They turned away from me and held council.

After a few moments, they turned to face me to deliver their verdict as one of them radioed the police. Pouya and Ali pleaded for their mercy with an urgency in their voices that frightened me. The police arrived, escorted me to the park station, and here I sat now, before the chief, with the boys outside the door waiting.

"Where are you from?" the police chief had asked.

"I was born here, but grew up in America."

"And how long have you been back in Tehran?"

"I arrived three days ago. It is my first time returning since I left as a child." I kept my eyes down, afraid he might be able to see that I was the kind of girl who participated, partially nude, in sweat hut ceremonies with strangers.

"Perhaps you do not understand the importance of modesty, having lived in America for so long?" the police chief said. "Perhaps the lewd ways of America seem normal to you?"

"I'm sorry," I said. "I thought the long skirt hid my ankles. I didn't mean to offend anybody."

He continued to lecture me for a long time on the importance of a girl's modesty. Perhaps he thought of himself as a benevolent father, teaching the prodigal daughter returned to her homeland after years and years of growing up in the midst of unrestrained sin. While he spoke in that hot office, I thought back to the sweat hut. I had sat there very immodestly, nearly naked, in the dark, among complete strangers, chanting and swaying, waiting for the visions, for clarity, for the point where the body hits a certain threshold and breaks open to the untethered flight of the conscious mind. I didn't achieve that in the sweat hut, though. Instead, I had sat there, too, trying to ignore the smell of all those bodies crowded into that tiny space. I felt relieved when the ceremony ended and we crawled back out into the yard. I lay belly down in the cool grass, picked the small daisies that grew there and wove them into a garland for my hair while the rest of the sweat hut cohort stared blissfully at the magnificent orange sunset.

Then, it got too cold to be outside naked, and we all went in for a potluck dinner. That's when the shaman started to speak, without pause, in a sort of trance. She talked about the great feminine spirit and the imbalance of the world. She talked about how, soon, a great battle would be waged between the feminine and the masculine energies, because the masculine spirit had dominated for too long, grown too immense, and in his hunger for power, he had swallowed forests, consumed whole oceans, left behind in his wake wasted earth and life, poisoned waters and air, death and destruction. This energy needed to be tempered, reeled in, soothed. I listened to her, practically hypnotized, until I shook myself out of that trance, realized it was late night already, thanked her, bade farewell to my yoga teacher, put on my clothes and drove home to pack my bags for my upcoming trip to Iran.

"Do you understand, then, what my job is, what I must do?" The police chief now asked me. "My job is to protect you. To keep you pure. So that when you stand before the gates of paradise, you will be granted admittance."

I kept my head down. I couldn't breathe. The scent of him. I wanted it to stop. The threat of him. His words. The shame he wanted me to feel. The smallness. Everything in me fought against him, but the battle was waged silently. If I wanted to walk out of this office, unharmed, I had to swallow my anger, my indignation. I had to choke back my words. I had to allow this humiliation into me, just deep enough for him to feel appeased. He sat, now, at the edge of his desk, right in front of me, looking down on my bowed head. The walls felt as though they were closing in. If I looked up, I'd see him. The portrait. The leer of the eyes.

"Do you understand that what we do is for your own good, young lady?"

I nodded. And that nod, the simple gesture of it, felt like blasphemy, a betrayal of myself. In fear of his power and his reach, I had handed him my dignity. Without a fight. But where would that fight have led me? I had heard the horror stories of what they did to young women. The assaults, the beatings, the imprisonment. I closed my eyes. To shut out that room, I tried to return to that backyard in Encino, the cool grass, the orange sunset. He sat there reading the minutiae of my gestures, watching closely, smelling the gentle break of my will, the softening of my hold. I could feel his pleasure. He chuckled.

"I can see that you feel remorse, that it was an error born of your ignorance. I will allow you to leave, this time," he said, satiated.

I stood up.

He leaned in toward me, close enough that the heat of his breath fell on the skin of my face and said, "But if you ever end up in my office again, I will not be so lenient with you."

Outside, Pouya and Ali waited for me. When I stepped into the sunlight, they ran up to me with concern. "What happened?" they asked. I shook my head. I wasn't ready to speak. I held the bitterness in my mouth. My body didn't feel like my own.

"Let's go play tennis. You'll feel better after," Ali said.

I didn't play with them, that afternoon. I sat beneath the shade of a tree and watched them play instead. The ease with which they moved. Their laughter. The freedom of their voices. They were boys, and while the laws restricted their freedoms, too, the whole machinery of the state seemed to be designed to break the spirit of women. The women needed to be controlled. And Ali knew this when he told me to put on his socks. Knew that they wanted to see his power, his domination. My weakness. My subservience.

I took my notebook out of my satchel and opened it under the shade of that tree. I sharpened the edge of my words, fashioned the tilt, and wrote the voice of that naked girl, the one I had hidden from the gaze of the police chief. She stood before the gates of his paradise, a garland of daisies in her hair, and let out a howl of rage that rattled those bars and shook their chains.

A WEEK AFTER my arrival, I met Sarab. He was sitting on the ledge of the flat rooftop of a house built of burnt red earth in a desert of the same red earth that stretched endless, at the moment when the sun was already sinking, so everything was cast in the ember glow of dusk, and on the edge above the distant mountains, a swath of blue and the faint glow of stars already in the sky.

The house was built by a famous artist whose daughter, Sanam, was courting Pouya with the intensity of a tiger. The first time I met Sanam, she walked into Behrooz's apartment wearing a blue headscarf. Sky blue. Color was a thing that stuck out in the streets of Tehran, among all that gray and black and dust and soot. Color was like one of those rogue flowers that managed to grow in the crack of the sidewalk, improbable, a defiant will to be beautiful, despite the ugliness of the concrete. And there was Sanam, just walking in off the street into our apartment, her sky blue headscarf covering the locks of her chestnut hair, strands of it in her face.

"Where did you get that color?" I asked her, since most of the scarves sold in the markets were muted tones, tans, browns, black.

"I saw it hanging in the bazaar on my way here," she said. "Blowing in the wind."

I imagined Sanam standing there, looking at that silk scarf billowing out like a piece of the sky tied around the hook from the bazaar seller's awning. I imagined her pointing to it, digging into the pocket of her jeans for the money, smoothing the crumpled bills out for the man, then brazenly taking off her own brown scarf, right there in the middle of the marketplace, with her hair revealed for the brief moment before she covered it again with her new scarf. I fell in love with her right then, with the color she brought in.

When we arrived at the house Sanam's father had built in the desert, Pouya turned to me and said, "There are two people here you should meet. One's a musician and the other guy is a photographer." We found Sanam poolside and followed her up a narrow, open staircase to the rooftop where Sarab sat on the very ledge, beside Shervin and Ramin, the three of them smoking, waiting for the first stars to appear.

Ramin the photographer and Shervin walked over to greet us, but Sarab stood in the peripheries. Then, slowly, he worked his way over and stood behind his two friends. Between Sarab and I there was already a violent magnetism, the kind of energy that exists between two dying stars. I didn't look at him, but I could feel him studying me. Finally, he entered our circle. A face full of angles. A thin, hard body. Sarab seemed always in motion, even when standing still. I caught his eyes. A dangerous depth in them.

"This is the musician I wanted you to meet," Pouya said.

"What do you play?" I asked.

"Guitar," Sarab said, hands deep in his pockets, toeing a nonexistent pebble with the tip of his Converse.

"I write and perform poetry," I said.

"You should perform one for us," Ramin the photographer said.

I wasn't shy about the performance of my poems. Back in Los Angeles, and then in San Francisco and Berkeley, I used to go to poetry readings and slams in coffee shops and theaters. I never talked about my father, his illness and death, or my relationship with Justin, or much of anything else with anybody, but on stage, in front of an audience of strangers, I would let go a whole flood of words. It felt cathartic. I decided to read my most recent poem for them, the one dedicated to that police chief. Without much preamble, I took my notebook from my satchel and read with all of the rage I had felt in that cloistered office, beneath the gaze of that man.

I finished the poem with the assertion that the gate to Paradise lay between my thighs, closed my book, and waited. The air had turned to the delicate, glasslike coolness that follows dry, inescapable heat. It was dark now. Maybe there was a moon, I can't remember. But if there was, let's say it was a yellow crescent.

Sarab said, "If you ever want to jam, call me."

Sarab lived in an apartment in the Gheytarieh district, coincidently the same neighborhood I had lived in as a child, before my family fled to America. I used to play on that very street, and even though I grew up in the quiet, sprawling isolation of the LA suburbs, Sarab's street, crowded with apartment buildings, held the ghosts of my childhood. When I finally reached his apartment and pushed the buzzer of the intercom for the first time, I felt like I had *arrived*.

I walked up three flights of stairs. The door to that home was already ajar. I took off my shoes, stepped in onto the cool tiled floors and aged rugs, closed the door and removed my hijab. A soft light filtered through reed blinds. On the floor were deep cushions. A large porcelain bowl rested by the wall, glazed a cobalt blue and chipped, filled with water and a handful of goldfish. There were books everywhere. Musical instruments, too. Each object in that small home looked as though it was placed with intention. Nothing was complacent. Sarab's mother, Raya, greeted me. She was thin, petite, spry. Her hair shaved to a stubble, then dyed silver. Raya was a staunch feminist and a single mother. She wrote articles and translated academic texts to make ends meet. She was fiercely critical. No nonsense. Easy to dance. Kids would come from all over the city to share their work with her. She took me under her wing immediately, and welcomed me into her home. "The boys are in Sarab's room," she told me.

When I walked into the room, Sarab, Shervin, and a handful of young musicians I didn't know were smoking and improvising. I didn't introduce myself to them or wait for an invitation. I sat down in their circle, the only girl among them, opened my notebook, and started to read. We played for a long while. Then, we cracked open a watermelon, put on an album, and let the afternoon sit with us. We roamed through ideas together. Laughed. Argued. Then played music, again.

The streets of Tehran were a fantastic stage for humanity, full of irony and tragedy, the comic and the absurd. And Sarab's home soon became my refuge. There, I could take the onslaught of experience and howl it out through poetry. Or dissect it, lay it bare, and make sense of it, then piece it back together. That home was a hallowed place, a thoughtful pause in all the madness, the sorrow, the raging summer heat that ravaged the city outside. It was where we gathered to create, and to be.

One afternoon, on my way to Sarab's house, I took a detour through the covered passageways of Bazaar Tajrish. I walked beneath a large dome in the middle of the bazaar. There was no one there, save a single figure. At first sight, he appeared as a crumpled mass of fabric someone had forgotten on the pavement. But then the jolt of electricity charged through his thin body, his bald head hitting the pavement with force, over and over, his back arching, his legs, his arms, flailing. He was the only motion in that marketplace. Everyone else had already scurried away, or stood still, in the shadows, watching.

When I realized what was happening, I ran to him, fell to my knees and held his head in my arms. I screamed for help until he fell still. Then, from somewhere in the shadows, from one of the storefronts, a man's voice said, "Don't concern yourself too much, Miss. He is probably putting on a show so people will take pity and throw him some pocket change."

I looked at his soot-covered face, eyes shut, bearded jaw clenched, foam and blood on his mouth. He was one of those men who sold coal from a sack he carried on his back from morning to night. He wore a shirt that may have been white once, and a suit that was black once, and perhaps fit him when he had more flesh on his bones. When the tremors started again, I panicked and cried louder for help.

Two young men stepped out of the shadows. They helped me pull him to the side and leaned him against a wall. After the gallant young men exited, the shadows in doorways, corners, windows dispersed. The bustling crowd resumed. Now, masses of people came and went, pinched fruit and held out lengths of silk fabric. Against a gray wall, on pavement littered with trash, the man, perhaps in his fifties, but so emaciated it was hard to tell, sat. His body shook from time to time. When he finally seemed to come back from that place of death, I asked, "Can I get you something?"

From around the corner, an old woman, an opium addict who sold miniature Korans, stepped into the light. She said,

"Hot tea. He needs hot tea with plenty of sugar. Follow me, I'll take you to where you can buy it."

I hurried after the old woman, since both age and addiction didn't seem to have much effect on her ability to maneuver with speed through the crowds and down the passageways.

"You shouldn't sit beside him." She came to a stop. "Buy his tea, and a cup for me, the guide."

"Why shouldn't I sit beside him?" I asked.

"Because then everyone will think you are of ill repute. Buy him some bananas, too. And he could probably use a Koran, for protection." She reached into a pocket somewhere beneath the fabric of her chador and held out a selection of miniature Korans in the palm of her hand.

"Don't let the old hag pull one over on you," the banana dealer said. "She smokes that money. Been here for years, now, and I've never seen her eat a bite of food."

I bought two Korans and handed one to the banana dealer. We finally came back to the epileptic coal seller, who sat and watched the passing crowd. I handed him the cup of tea, and the old woman disappeared, like smoke.

As it had become customary with me whenever I met someone in dire need in those streets and felt overwhelmed by the guilt of my own privilege, I took all the money I carried and put it in a small pile of crumpled bills and coins beside the bananas. I looked around. A faceless stream of people passed by. I thought for a moment about what the old woman had said, then sat down beside that man anyway. I remembered the miniature Koran and gave it to him, too. The coal seller looked at me, in my saffron headscarf and blue jeans. Then, he took a sip of the tea, closed his eyes, and rested his head back on the wall. With his eyes closed, he recited a passage from the Koran about how, even when we think there are no witnesses, even in total darkness, Allah watches our doings and takes them into account.

I told him about America, about my father, about his death and the day I opened my eyes, and saw the beauty. He told me how he was once a proud man, a veteran of the army, and how, in his youth, he knew how to detonate a bomb that could bring down a whole building in seconds. I asked him why in the world would he want to do such a thing. He paused and thought for a minute, then shrugged his shoulders and said, "It was what we were told to do."

We sat for a while longer, in silence. Then he turned to me and said, "It isn't safe for you to sit here like this, with me. People will think badly of you." He rose slowly to his feet, put the crumpled bills and coins in his back pocket, put the miniature Koran in his breast pocket, held the bananas in his hand and the sack of coal in the other, and walked away, into the bustle of the gray crowd.

Later, at Sarab's apartment, I told Raya what had happened, how no one stepped forward to help. "They've witnessed that sort of tragedy daily, for years and years," she said. "You are only audience to it. You can leave at will. You can afford to watch his suffering. You have the luxury to feel pity. The rest of us, we need to keep going."

·　·　·

77

UNCLE BEHROOZ DECIDED it was finally time to leave
the heat and the congestion of the city and go into the wilderness, trekking. Since this would be my first trek with them,
he wanted to see how fit I was with a trial journey, a single
day's walk and camp overnight in a valley he knew right outside of Tehran.

The morning of our trip, before the bus arrived, I waited
outside of Behrooz's apartment with my hair done up in a
bunch of little braids and my Das Meindl boots laced up. I
had bought those boots in Canada on my first trip out of the
United States on my own. The sales guy in Vancouver told
me about the boots' three-hundred-year history, showed me
pictures of archaeologists in the field wearing them, and said
they could carry me to first base camp on Mount Everest
without trouble. I imagined myself standing beside my handsome sherpa, my cheeks red from the cold, the flap of the
tent behind us slapping in the wind and the sun setting in the
distance. For the sake of keeping all future possibilities
open, I shelled out the four hundred bucks to pay for the
boots, which I wore on several trips throughout the Pacific
Northwest, and now I intended to tread the soil of Iran with
them, too. I stood beside my backpack, meticulously packed
with not a sock more than what I'd need, ready to meet any
challenge.

All the members of our party arrived, save for Amir,
Pouya's friend from the university where they had both studied architecture. I didn't know, when Amir's cab finally
arrived, that he would come to play such a prominent role in
my undoing. But throughout my days in Iran, Amir was

always in the background, on trekking trips, at parties, informal gatherings. He was among a handful of boys vying for my attention. And he always followed me, silently, constantly, like a shadow. That morning, he put his pack on the ground and paid the cab driver. Then he turned, looked at me, ran a hand through his black hair, and smiled a dazzling smile.

When we arrived at the foothills of the Alborz mountains, Behrooz paid the driver and told him to return to pick us up the following afternoon. I stood beside my uncle and looked at that mountain with apprehension. After a few moments of silence, he said to me, "You look at the peak, once, just to tell yourself it's there. Then you start walking, slow and steady. And you love each step. You love the flowers you see, the rocks. You love your body, and the way it hurts and how it achieves, and before you know it, you will arrive."

Then, he started walking up the trail.

"Follow me," he said. "Match my pace and my breathing."

I walked behind him. Behind the tall, strong, reassuring bulk of him. I walked slow and steady, and breathed slow and steady. Every now and then, he'd reach his hand back without looking and give me a date, or a handful of walnuts. Often, he sang. The rest of the kids walked and chatted, but I followed Behrooz diligently. Until we reached the summit and there, beneath the open skies, Behrooz turned to me and said, "You have the spirit of a mountaineer."

I stood there on that mountain, the whole of it covered in wildflowers, and felt so powerful. I was tired, my feet hurt, my back ached, and nobody but me knew about my heart condition, the prognosis of the defect, but I had scaled that peak, nonetheless. I felt invincible. Then, our party descended into the green lap of a valley.

After that first night of camping, of singing and dancing beside a roaring fire, Ali there, and Sanam, a handful of other kids, and Amir, watching me silently, I awoke in my tent to the sound of bells and baaing. I stepped out, groggy eyed, to find myself in a sea of goats, and amongst those goats, the cowboys of Iran. Mustached Reza, a proud shepherd with the big, white mustache he was known for, stood beside his seven sons, surrounded by their tremendous herd of goats. He was greeting my uncle. Behrooz and Mustached Reza were old friends, and Mustached Reza told his sons to milk some of the goats for his honored guests.

The goats lined up for those shepherd sons like orderly schoolgirls, and one by one, with uncanny speed, the sons pulled on their udders and the milk hit the tin pail with a force that zinged and steamed. Every so often, some excited goat dropped a few pellets into the bucket, too. Seemed that shepherds had a five-second rule, with one hand still milking, the sons scooped out the feces with the other. Those muscled, rosy-cheeked shepherd boys took that fresh, steaming milk in the metal pail and heated some over an open fire, then mixed in crystalized Nescafé coffee and served it to us in tin cups, in the middle of a valley in the lap of the Alborz mountain range, with the grass covered in dew and the mist just rising.

After that initial trip, when Behrooz saw that I was sturdy enough to take on mountains, he planned a longer, more challenging journey, a two-day trek starting in a village just outside of Tehran, then through the mountains, and ending in a northern village, inaccessible by car, known for its untouched beauty. The minute we got off the bus in the village of Taleghan, our backpacks strapped to our backs, ready for the trek through the wilderness and into the village of Deleer, a group of little boys crowded around us. It was a beautiful summer morning, bright, birds mad with song, profusion of flowers, tall grass, the air cool and crisp, the joyful chatter of those little boys with their sparkling eyes. An old woman walked in our direction. She wore a floral print dress over baggy turquois pants. In all that radiance, the old woman walked over the bridge that crossed a gurgling stream, past the bus, past every other member of our party, through the crowd of little boys, who parted respectfully for her, and she stopped in front of me. Then, she placed her aged hand right on my belly and looked me directly in the eyes.

"What have you come seeking?" She asked.

I knew enough about the culture of Iran to know that old women were ascribed with a special kind of magic. Old and wise, they were said to be powerful. I wasn't partial to superstition, but I wasn't about to trample centuries-old beliefs without a little tact, either.

"Only to walk through the mountains, mother," I said. "With your permission." I would have liked to share a cup of tea with her in her home, beside her hearth, and listen to her stories.

"From where are you coming?" she asked.

"America," I said.

She nodded. We stood beside each other in silence for a while. I watched the boys climb on top of one another's shoulders to nail a banner from the top of one telephone pole to another, each critiquing the previous boys' techniques. Someone must have entrusted these little boys with this rather dangerous task, handed them nails and hammer, and instructed them to hang banners from the top of telephone poles for an upcoming event. They took it very seriously. The eldest, who couldn't have been more than eight, assumed the role of leader. My uncle spoke to the bus driver, then paid him. The rest of the members of our group readied themselves to leave. Somewhere in the distance came the jangle of bells from a flock of sheep. An old man ushered a mule past us, loaded with an impossible burden of sticks.

The old woman finally spoke.

"I, too, came from far away," she said. "I was a girl when my husband brought me over these mountains from the village where I was born. I have known these mountains, walked them, become like them. Many seasons I have seen in these mountains. Not many more seasons before I return to them."

Then, she held my arm, came in real close to my face and said, "You will see the face of death, my child, but G.d walks with you. Listen for Him in the mountains. Go. Walk without fear." She placed a finger on my forehead, then turned away and began walking back to the cluster of earth-plastered homes beyond the wooden bridge that crossed the gurgling stream.

Back during the Iran-Iraq War in the eighties, while my family became refugees in America, Behrooz and his young family stayed in Tehran and left for the wilderness whenever the bombings became heavy. He'd pack up the family, his little boys and his wife, and set off for the mountains. Snow or shine. They lived in the quiet of nowhere while fire rained down on the cities. When the planes stopped droning overhead, they'd walk back into the city and resume life in their home, the kids returned to school, and Behrooz went back to being an architect, not too profitable a career when buildings were being reduced to rubble regularly.

He used to send us pictures, along with letters he wrote in a code our family had devised so that we could communicate with one another without arousing the suspicions of the agents who opened the letters or listened in on the phone conversations that anything of importance was being exchanged. Mundane sentences like *"How much did you sell the TV for?"* meant *"Do you need money?"* And with these letters written in double-speak, Behrooz included photographs. His wife and the boys on the peak of a green mountain. The boys on skis in the snow. He and his wife reclining on tapestried pillows on thick rugs in the tents of Bakhtiari nomads in their encampments along a river.

The world I grew up in did not have nomads or missiles or encampments along a river. The world I knew was a suburb of orderly homes, one of two prototypes in a shade of tan with a green manicured lawn, with or without a pool, a repetition of this sameness that stretched endlessly toward oblivion. Two cars in the garage. Two kids, each in their own rooms. A multitude of TVs, air conditioning, washing machine, dryer, a dog, a cat, two-week vacations. Growing up in that American suburb as a kid, there was no wilderness. Even the future was mapped out, clearly. School. College. Career. Marriage.

Children. The repayment of debts, followed by retirement, probably in a home for the old, lonely, forgotten. Death.

It had been Behrooz's stories, far and fantastic from the world I knew, that enticed me and had brought me back to Iran. Stories about avalanches, packs of wolves, of being lost and surviving with nothing more than your wits and your desire to live. After my father's death, I could feel the muffled angst inside all those suburban homes surrounding ours. The boredom. The rage. We were all like a bunch of caged gorillas, pounding against the glass in fits of desperation, knowing that, somewhere, there existed something more than just this tedious comfort. And something in me hollered for that wilderness. Something in me bellowed for an unknown freedom.

Of course, I appreciated the fact that I didn't have to go to bed at night fearing imminent death by bomb, though I had a taste of that, briefly, as a child. The war began before my family escaped Iran, so I experienced the air-raid sirens, and the scrambling to the dark basements in the middle of the night, where the landlord's wife screamed that we were all about to die, while her husband tried to muffle her cries, and the rest of us, trembling, listened for the planes overhead. My first week at elementary school in America, there was an earthquake drill during lunch on the playground. I thought it was an air-raid siren. All the kids around me fell to the ground and covered their necks with their rumps in the air. I stood among all those ducking children and searched the cloudless blue skies until I spotted the airplane passing overhead. I didn't know how to scream, "Get up and find cover, you turkeys, they can see you!"

I assimilated. I pushed that knowing deep down into some hidden place in my psyche. I replaced those nights of terror with *Mister Rogers' Neighborhood* and *Sesame Street*. But there was more to my childhood in Tehran than terror. There was an entire world of joy I was forced to leave behind, too. My early childhood in Tehran was spent playing on the streets after school until dusk. All the kids of our neighborhood, right in the middle of the street, games of tag and soccer and hide and seek, explorations of gardens, discoveries, snowball fights, and sledding, riding our bikes, helmetless and haphazardly, planting in community gardens that sprang up in any vacant lot that wasn't fenced in. We knew all the adults on the street, and they knew us. Everyone watched out for everyone else.

The suburban streets of Los Angeles were deathly quiet in the afternoons, like those Westerns of ghost towns with tumbleweeds. All the kids sat inside, watching TV. Not interacting with real children or real adults, but experiencing that relationship as a viewer, behind a screen. Community was something that happened somewhere else, community as fictional storytelling. Even our tragedies were lived through the TV, only interrupted by commercial breaks. We didn't live, really. We watched.

But Behrooz had always lived in the quick of things. Death came raining down, and he took his children into the wilderness and taught them how to keep living. And when the war came to an end, and the Islamic theocracy managed a chokehold on the Iranian people, Behrooz watched his kids grow up strangled by this new regime and started taking whole groups of kids out into the wilderness. He took his teenage boys and their friends into the mountains, trekking, where they could shed the hijab, ignore the Islamic laws, the instilled fear, and live freely, if only for a moment, in nature with nothing more than the bare necessities and their own will to be. So, when he came to America and found me off-kilter, he invited me to Iran to participate in these journeys.

It took a while for me to realize that I needed to accept that invitation. One day, at work in the high-rise beside the CNN building, I was finalizing the subtitling files of some horror film. It was the deadline for that project, but one of the scenes in the film still needed synching. In that scene, a young woman, scantily clad in a bikini, sat in a hot tub before a man broke in upon her, tried to kill her with a power drill, which ultimately fell into the water and electrocuted her to death. I watched this scene twenty-five times, checking the dialogue in twenty-five languages, and that was when I realized the utter futility of my work. I had just witnessed my father die a long, slow, devastating death. How could I squander the life given to me? What was I doing at this desk? So I completed that project, walked to the human resources office, and told them I quit.

Now I was standing here, in this little village tucked into a valley in the midst of the Alborz mountains, and an old woman, a village elder, had just placed her hand on my belly and read the signs, then touched my forehead and commanded me to walk bravely forth into the wilderness.

And wilderness trekking in Iran was not easy. There were no trails. There were no kindly rangers or little trail books to sign your name and write a message. There were no signs mentioning if you were on the right path, no developed drinking spouts for water, and if you got lost or stuck hanging from the side of a cliff, no search-and-rescue team would come to save you. There were, however, shepherds strewn here and there with their flock of sheep or goats. Other than that, it was a vast desolation, a reckoning with your own mortality.

After the old woman's blessing, we started out of the village. Behrooz headed the team and Pouya brought up the rear. Behrooz studied topographic maps and knew how to find freshwater springs. Our route followed this path, from spring to spring, with Behrooz as our chief. Behrooz was a Jewish man living in a predominately Muslim country and, more often than not, a country hostile toward Jews and other religious minorities. The people who participated in the treks he led were mostly Muslim. And they loved Behrooz. Adored him, respected him, entrusted their lives to him and learned from him. This was a narrative often kept from the Western audience, the love and respect and friendship that existed between Muslims and Jews, so that when we heard that such a thing happened, when we saw it, it came as something of a shock. Sure, the strife between the two parties was real, but it was also the only story we were told. So here's another story, to add to the collective narratives of the East . . .

Once upon a time, in Iran, a Jewish man took a crowd of Muslim kids under his wing and led an exodus of them out of the tomb of the city and into the wilderness, where the kids laughed and walked and breathed in freedom, where they found themselves and the strength and the courage to walk back into that city without losing the beautiful glimmer of hope that sustains the human soul.

And what a pretty wilderness it was. Tall, green mountains. Rushing rivers. Wildflowers all over. We climbed to summits, climbed down from summits, climbed to other summits. By sunset, we arrived at our first camp, at the top of a mountain, which plateaued in a grassy field full of irises. In the center of this plateau was a beautiful, blue lake. A German seismologist and his Iranian guide and their cute little donkey loaded with supplies had already set up camp. The Alborz mountains have a record of significant seismic activity, and this guy had come out to study them. He was handsome, in a Germanic way, and he came up to our group, not speaking a word of English, which all the kids spoke, and the only way he could communicate was through the translations of his Iranian guide. The German made it known right away that he had been "dry" for quite a spell, and would we be kind enough to share some of our wine with him? Soon, we were all drinking beside a blazing fire, singing "Hotel California" beneath the stars that sparkled overhead.

In the Islamic Republic of Iran, alcohol is illegal. If someone is caught with it, unless they can afford a very handsome bribe to the police, the prison ward, and the judge, they can expect a minimum of eighty lashes from a whip. In the old days, the Jews and the Armenians, who were exempt from the prohibition of alcohol, made their own wine and sometimes

sold it to Muslim patrons, in secret. Uncle Behrooz had carried on the tradition of making wine. Each year, at the near-
end of the grape season, he'd send his sons to the fruit bazaar
to buy crates and crates of grapes, and the boys disinfected
the bathtub and invited friends to mash these grapes.

Pouya believed that the wine, both its taste and its potency,
was directly linked to who stepped on the grapes, their mood
and thoughts at the time, the combination of the people in the
tub, and their particular relationships to one another, so he
carefully orchestrated the whole thing. That summer I made
wine with them, we played Miles Davis's "Bitches Brew," and
read out loud from Omar Khayyám's poetry, and drank wine
from the previous year straight from the bottle. Pouya swore,
the following year, that the bottles from that barrel led to a
terrifying and exhilarating drunkenness. Behrooz's apartment building was situated between a mosque and a Bureau
of Intelligence. The Intelligence building had a floodlight on
the rooftop that shone right into Uncle Behrooz's apartment.
Meanwhile, the mosque was always celebrating the birth or
the death of this or that imam, with amplified chanting and
chest beating, and with the comings and the goings of the
devout. To be in a tub full of grapes with Miles Davis playing,
surrounded by the police and dead imams, it was terrifying,
and it was exhilarating.

After a few more rounds of "Hotel California" interspersed
with attempts at ballads by Metallica with the German beside
the fire, one by one, we retired to our tents and fell into a deep
sleep. When we awoke, the seismologist had already packed
and left, and there were two large billy goats sitting on either

side of Behrooz as he sipped his morning tea and watched the mist rising from the valley below. A shepherd showed up to collect his billy goats and he told us there was a faster path to our next stop, Amoorok, a little encampment on a river where a large family of nomads lived with their sheep in the summer months. The shepherd pointed us in that direction and swore it would get us there in two hours' time, instead of the full day hike we had planned. Behrooz took him at his word, and we changed our route.

It was not that the shepherd was dishonest. His reality was different from the common man's. He lived in the open, beneath the bare skies. He drank the milk of his goats, and sometimes ate the flesh. He watched for wolves, and slept among dogs just as fierce. And his idea of a path was a goat's idea of a path. His feet were trained differently, his sense of danger, of falling off a cliff, of rockslides, these instincts were totally different from ours. Perhaps he could have walked that day's hike in a couple of hours. But we couldn't. In fact, after several hours of walking, the sun ready to set, we still hadn't reached our destination. We stood in the middle of nowhere. Lost.

That night, I sat at the top of a rocky mountain, leaning against a ruined hovel, a couple walls of rocks kept in place by mud that, maybe a hundred years ago, served as some poor shepherd's shelter against the elements. We had made a fire and heated up the last of our food. There wasn't much singing. We were all pensive, and we watched the shooting stars overhead quietly until we retired to our tents to sleep.

Morning came. Behrooz boiled up a bit of bulgur wheat he kept at the bottom of his pack for emergencies, and we each ate a spoonful. Our water bottles were pretty low, and we didn't know when or where we'd find clean water again. We started walking. By noon, we were a haggard bunch. It didn't feel like trekking anymore. Now, it was a downright fight to survive. Our bodies were fatigued, thirsty, hungry, and I was the weakest link in the whole group. Behrooz asked Pouya to stay behind and walk with me, while the rest forged ahead to find a way off that mountain.

There we were, on the top of a very high mountain, at the edge of which was a very sharp cliff, and the distance between where we walked and where things fell off into the abyss was very little. At one point, I accidentally kicked a stone. It tumbled twice and disappeared off the ledge. Just like that, one tumble, two, and gone forever into the unknown.

That's when I froze. I could not take another step forward. I was done. I stood there, beneath that mercilessly hot sun, and then collapsed into a little heap. Pouya came strolling up to me and said, "Let me carry some of your stuff."

Funny thing, ego. Even though I was convinced that I was dying, no hyperbole, I mean I was literally dying, I believed that my pack was a metaphor for the burden I was meant to carry in life, and no one but I could bear that weight, so I said, "No. I can do it."

Pouya knelt down, looked me in the eyes, and said, "Sometimes, you have to give others the opportunity to do good, too."

And that was a good enough argument for me. I really did need to work on trusting others, and being close to falling to my death felt as good a time as any to start. He emptied my pack into his, placed the empty bag back on my shoulders, and helped me to my feet. But still. Despite my trusty Das Meindl boots, which the salesman had assured me would carry me through any situation, my feet refused to walk. Some synapse between my brain and my feet had snapped, and the command to walk just didn't reach my heals any longer.

Standing there, I remembered my mother on the day of my father's death. During the three years of my father's illness, my mother slept on the floor beside his bed. She bathed him, dressed him, fed him, searched the world for a cure that might help him, prayed for him, wept with him, carried him when he couldn't walk anymore. I was never home, and when I was, I was unpredictable and angry.

In the early stages of my father's illness, I prayed a lot. I prayed when he started holding my hand to steady himself. I prayed when he started using a walker. I prayed when he became wheelchair bound. I prayed when his speech started to slur, when I heard him weeping behind the closed bedroom door. Finally, when he lost the ability to speak, I stopped praying and turned to threats, instead . . . I told G.d that if He took my father, I'd kill myself, too. And then came the morning when my father died.

Three days previously, my father's breathing had become more strained. I knew that ALS often ended like this, that the person suffocates. But I wouldn't admit to myself it was happening. I stayed home and sat at the dining table, listening to my father struggling to breathe, and I busied myself with a research paper I was writing for school. I woke up in the middle of that night, before the morning of his death and I walked to his room to check on him. He labored to breathe in his sleep. I went back to bed, fell asleep and dreamed about him. I hadn't dreamed about my father in three years, but he was there, in my dreams on that last night, and I had my arms around his neck, and I cried and cried, and a fantastic light shone all around him, and he laughed.

I asked him, through my tears, "What am I going to do now?" And he said, "You are going to live your life."

That morning, around 7:30 a.m., as I drove to the community college that I was attending, a cool breeze came in through my open car window and I took a sip from the Styrofoam cup of tea I had purchased from a gas station and, suddenly, I experienced a jarring memory, a strong familiarity of that exact moment with tea, morning sunlight through windshield, cool breeze with the smell of the ocean on it. I had already lived this moment, it was both memory and the present, at once. But this wasn't my own memory that I was reexperiencing. It was my father's memory. This is how he must have felt each morning when he left for work, when he could still work. He sipped his tea and felt the pleasure of the morning air on his face as he drove, knowing that his wife and his daughter slept in their warm beds at home.

I knew, in that moment, that my father was living, feeling this experience through me. And I knew, after that moment, that he was no longer alive.

I drove back home blindly, weeping, screaming, pleading for him to wait for me. It was the first of May, and wild narcissus grew near the coastal hills. Those were his favorite flowers. I wept and screamed and told him to wait, because I hadn't brought him narcissus this spring, I hadn't brought him a bunch of narcissus to put beside his bed, so that he could smell them, so that he could see their delicate, paper-white beauty. "Wait," I screamed and drove blindly down the winding canyons that led home. "Wait and I will bring you all the damned flowers from all these damned hills." I parked the car in the driveway, ran to the door and pounded until my mother opened it.

I asked, "Where is my father?"

And she said, "He is gone."

I turned and walked back to the car, because G.d and I had a deal, if he took my father from me, I'd commit suicide. And this was it, the time had come. I was going get into that car, drive the way I had come, and drive right off a cliff.

My mother followed behind me and asked, "Where are you going?"

"Nowhere."

"Please . . . Don't leave me."

I don't know why I turned back, but I did. I turned to tell her where I intended to go, and I saw her. I mean, I *saw* her. I saw her pain, and her beauty in that pain. I saw that she was the manifestation of love and light, entrapped in a human body. My heart broke open, and the world flooded in and drowned me. And now, here I was, frozen on the edge of a cliff in Iran, with death right before me, and I remembered my mother asking, "Where are you going?"

There was a prayer she sang beside my father's open grave. She had sat down beside the earth that his brothers and friends would shovel on his coffin, on the very edge of that abyss, and she sang a prayer. It was the sunlight and it was the wind and it was earth. It was all of the beauty and all of the sorrow of the living. With my feet turned to rocks and the nothingness so near, the echo of that song my mother had sung years before somehow managed to travel through time and space to find me where I stood now, turned to stone from fear and fatigue, and that prayer sent an electrifying jolt right from the crown of my head to the soles of my tired, begrudging feet. I started walking, and I started singing loudly enough for my mother to hear me, and she must have heard me while sitting on the edge of her husband's grave, and she must have sung her prayer loud enough for it to reach me both then and now, in this time when I needed strength to see past the fear, past the face of death, so that I could walk forth.

Pouya strolled quietly behind me, looking off into the distance, giving me the space I needed to reckon with whatever I needed to reckon with, until we finally turned around a bend and saw Behrooz sitting with the rest of the group, listening. Below us stretched a visible valley. And in that distant valley, the thin ribbon of a river.

We finally came to a slope we could walk down, made up of loose rocks. Those rocks came alive with motion each time we moved so that with every step, we slid forward several feet. At any moment, our descent could have triggered a rock slide that would have crushed and buried us. We walked slowly, slid, held our breaths. We were hit by rocks that came hurtling at us, left us bruised, scraped, bleeding.

During the walk down that treacherous mountain, Javid kept saying, over and over, "You have no idea how many miracles have befallen you each minute that passes. No idea what a miracle it is to be alive." He said this with a tone of humor and perhaps irony, but he was right. Each step that didn't bury us was a miracle. And there came, finally, the most miraculous moment, when we found ourselves at the foot of that mountain, a few yards from the banks of that river we had seen from the top of the cliff. That thin ribbon of water in the far, green valley now rushed before us. Behrooz walked slowly to the bank, then sat. He had delivered us. Safely. He boiled some water for us to drink before we started to walk again, following the river toward the encampment of Amoorok, where a large shepherd family stayed during the summer months.

After an hour's walk, we saw their tents. There must have been thousands of sheep there, surrounding a group of men engaged in a very serious conversation. They were all relatives and they were discussing who would take their flocks where in search of grass. When they saw our group, dust-covered, visibly haggard, cut and bleeding, they stopped immediately and approached us. Behrooz told them the ordeal, and a couple of the men hurried to bring us a large, tin pail of fresh yogurt. The head of the tribe told us to go to his tent and ask his wife for bread.

We were complete strangers to them. They lived in these mountains because it was their home. They searched for green pastures as a matter of survival. We risked our lives for sport. We lived in nice city apartments, with running hot water and electricity and fridges full of food. They thought of winters and wolves and droughts. We came out of the mountains, hungry and lost, and they welcomed us into their fold, despite our strangeness.

Outside the flap of the largest tent, we asked if we could enter. A woman's voice welcomed us in. Only the girls of our group walked into her home. The men waited outside, respectfully. The mistress of the house was a beautiful young woman, her black hair held back by a colorful headscarf, her skin freckled, her cheeks rosy, her body lean and strong. She was probably the same age we were, but already had a toddler at her skirt and a baby at her breast. She stood in the middle of that large, round tent, where there was a makeshift stove over an open flame. Above it, in the ceiling of the tent, was an opening that allowed in light and let out smoke. The floors of that home were of earth, but earth watered and tamped down, so that there was no dust. A warm, soft light filtered in, and all around the canvas walls were wool cushions and bedding in rich colors rolled up to serve as couches.

"Are you hungry?" she asked.

And I burst into tears. I wept, uncontrollably, silently, and looked at her. She went to where she kept the bread she baked each day, wrapped in cloth to keep it fresh, and she unwrapped it and handed that bread to me. And I wept some more. She turned to one of the girls in our group and asked, "Why is your friend crying so much?"

And that girl replied, "She is from America."

I suppose that was the reason. In a way. Because I had never felt welcome. Because the doors of all those homes in that suburban neighborhood of Los Angeles always remained shut. And here I stood in a dirt-floored tent, hungry and tired and lost and scared, and she had welcomed me in, then shared with me her family's daily bread.

The last leg to the village of Deleer was a three-hour hike that followed the river. We arrived right before the sun set. That village, in my memory, is beautiful beyond words. Remote, without any developed roads leading to it, tucked in the green northern mountains and hidden by lush forests. At the eastern entrance from the river stood an old walnut tree. She was a giant, and the villagers, for lack of a better word, revered her. Not in a pagan, ritualistic sense. She was just old and beautiful and, for generations, had provided the villagers with her fruit and her shade. She had presided over ancestors the villagers only knew from the tombstones in the cemetery, and would outlive them to see the great-grandchildren they themselves would never meet. The walnut tree was like a village elder. An ancient old woman who stood witness to the passage of time, and who cared for those who came to her. Anyone who entered the village from the east walked beneath her shade first.

The houses were made of earth and stone, the roofs thatched. Roses grew profusely, climbed the walls, around the windows, over the thresholds. The doors and the wood frames of the windows were painted in bold reds and blues, yellows, greens. Roosters of the same bold colors patrolled the narrow paths between the homes, and those paths wound up and down, past doors that were always open, and in those doorways stood women with rosy cheeks, or old and bent, or young and shy, or plump with motherhood, all inviting us in as we walked past them. They greeted us, told us what they had cooking on their hearths, and said, "Come in, share a meal with us."

Beside their doorways stood aluminum canisters that once held lard or coffee, now filled with soil and growing a profusion of cosmos and geraniums. Old men sat in the shade of trees, sipping tea and chatting with one another. Able-bodied men and women returned from the fields. I wept there, too, as I walked through that village at dusk. I walked and wept and the children followed me and asked where I had come from, and why I cried. I turned to Behrooz and asked, "Why can't we live like this? Why can't it be so simple and so pure?"

Behrooz looked at me and laughed. Then he ruffled my hair and said, "After one day, you would waste away from boredom. This is not a life for you."

I wanted it to be a life for me. I wanted to be a fisherman's wife. I wanted to have goats, live in a village, write poetry, and birth babies in my earthen home with its thatched roof and primitive wooden furniture. I wanted to cook stews in a cauldron on a wood-fueled stove. I wanted to make fresh butter and wash my clothes in a river against rocks. Why couldn't this be my life, in place of those suburbs back in Los Angeles, those identical houses with their manicured lawns, their washing machines, their two-car garages, treadmills, TVs, microwaves?

I was twenty-four, I had the power of choice but the heart of a child. It was a purely magnificent age. Everything was possible. I could choose any story I wanted my life to be, and in that evening, walking through the narrow paths of that village, I wanted to be simple and pure. I wanted to tear up the map I had been given in America, forgo the ease, the security, the stability of all that and live, instead, in the wilderness of those mountains of Northern Iran, and grow old in those mountains, and return to those mountains.

I imagine it, now, from time to time. I imagine myself there, despite all that has come to pass. After the falling of the towers, the burning of the cities, the explosions of madmen, the slaughtering of children, after the wasting away of the earth, after all this, televised and broadcast, headline after headline after headline, I imagine what that boredom might have been like, in that little lost village, beneath the protective shade of that ancient walnut tree.

Behrooz hired the only two cars in the whole village to take us back to Tehran. We drove over the narrow, bumpy, dirt road out of the mountains and to the main highway that led back to the city. When we reached the highway, our driver slipped in a cassette tape, the kind of drum and bass you might have heard in any nightclub in Europe in those days. He turned the music up, then drove like he wanted death. He raced the other hired car, swerved in and out of the opposite lane toward oncoming traffic, barely making it back into our lane, barely skirting the edge of a cliff that offered no barricades to keep us from flying right off. We screamed at him to slow down. We pleaded. We threatened not to pay. But he drove on, without heed. And Javid, who sat in the front seat of our car, his hands stretched out to the dashboard, kept yelling, and laughing, "You have no idea how many miracles have just passed this moment. You have no idea what a miracle it is to be alive."

.   .   .

WHEN WE RETURNED to Tehran, I was in love. I can't write an exhaustive list of what I was in love with, because I was in love with everything. I was in love with the taxi drivers. The surly ones. The quiet ones. The inquisitive. The ones who recited poetry. The ones who talked about their dreams. I was in love with the Kurdish men who stood on the side of the road tall and proud, with their thick mustaches and their baggy pants and the colorful scarves wound about their waists, who waited all day for someone to hire them. I was in love with the little boys who followed shoppers at the bazaar with their wheelbarrows, insisting. I was in love with the recording of the azaan broadcasted over the city from the tops of minarets at dawn, at midday, at dusk. The smell of hot piroshkis from the bakery, the colorful display of seasonal fruit, the hanging carcass of a goat, the dazed chicks that sold for pennies each, dyed hot pink and neon green and who lived for less than a day. I was in love with the merchants who napped in the late afternoons on the piled bags of wheat they sold, in the corner of their shops. I was in love with the beggars. In love with the street musicians. The prostitutes. With the policemen in their ill-fitting uniforms. With the butchers in their bloodstained white aprons. I was in love with the beautiful young women. In love with the young men. The old men. The tired mothers. The street sweepers who swept with brooms made of bramble. I was in love with the mullahs who walked in the shade of the elm trees that lined the streets and avenues, their cloaks billowing out behind them like sails. In love with the fruit dealers who sang about their produce, how ripe it was, how sweet it was, how cheap. I walked the streets in love. Delirious with love. Broken-hearted with love. Shining with love. Crazy with love. The sight of a mechanic's hands eternally covered in grease, or the purple hands of the man who sold roasted beets from a cart, or the blackened fingers of the young children who shelled raw walnuts and sold them on the corners moved me to tears. Iran. I was in love with Iran. All of her. Her sorrow, her suffering, her beauty, her strength. Her magic. Her spirit. She was mine, I was hers, this was love.

This madness, of course, drew a bit of attention in the streets. People noticed. But it inspired a kindness in strangers toward me, the way a community accepts a village idiot. And I wasn't afraid to be the fool. I was given to bouts of joy, of ecstatic gratuity to the world as it manifested. There, in the streets of Tehran, I walked enraptured, spellbound. The world was gifted to me. Gluttonous, I wanted all of it. I became engorged, every one of those taxi drivers my confidant, every fruit vendor my friend, every beggar my guilt, every old woman my mother, every argument my folly, every act of kindness, everything, mine. I felt like I was awakening, again, for the second time in my life from a deep sleep, and I stretched myself wide to encompass the whole of it. I felt the unfurling of my ego in every direction, through the winding passageways, down the wide avenues, over the tall garden walls, into the tight and narrow streets, into homes, alleys and high-rises, schools and offices and banks and stores. I had thousands of eyes, and thousands of mouths, and arms and legs and hearts and hopes. I was all of the immense humanity before me. I walked the streets with impunity, holding a bag of persimmons or apples, and handing them out to every beggar who crossed my path, to groups of day laborers and construction workers. Even the police gave me license as they watched this loudness of character, this fearlessness, this openness, and they let me be.

It was a happy time. Those days.

So my cousins and I decided to host a party, to share the happiness, the miracle of being alive. Behrooz had just moved the family from their old apartment in the quiet and secluded outskirts of Tehran into his new building in the heart of the city. The old apartment still stood vacant. Pouya and I searched the bazaars far and wide for black lights and hired a DJ with the right music. We soundproofed the home with egg cartons and blankets on the windows to muffle the bass so policemen passing in the streets below wouldn't hear us, and invited a whole bunch of people and gave them a password, and told them to dress outlandishly. I put on my white thrift-store hippie dress and wove myself a garland of daisies for my hair and fashioned some wings out of silk and wire, and the night of the party came, and the guests arrived and that's when Reza walked in through the door.

Reza, the One.

There were no formal introductions between Reza and me. I had my back turned when he walked in with his girl, his brother, and his gang of friends. But I felt him enter the room. Let me get this right. Forget form. For a moment. Forget the idea of two separate people in a room crowded with other people, a certain distance between them. Reduce everything down to the atomic, to the burning core surrounded by the dance of particles smaller than even that. There, the strict boundaries of the body dissipate, elements merge with one another, breath with the particles of air, feet with the seeming solidity of the ground, and in between all those dancing atoms, nothing exists but empty space. And energy. And heat. And attraction. In the minutia of that universe, some frequency, some taut vibration of strings pulled between Reza and me, and he looked over, past the crowd of bodies to where I stood, looking at him. Then, he looked away. And his girl, who had been his girl since they were children playing on the same street, felt that connection as a palpable threat and withdrew to another room, upset. In that same moment, Amir appeared out of nowhere and asked me to dance, and even when dancing with my eyes closed, in between so many bodies sweating and moving, amidst a concoction of dizzying pheromones, to the bewildering thump of the music, I still knew Reza's precise location in space, like the needle of a compass drawn north.

It was like that. Everything around us a shadow, a charade. The only thing that existed, that Existed, was whatever strange attraction pulled Reza and me, finally, to the center of that dancing crowd, to the apex of that gyrating storm, where he and I finally stood, facing one another. I stopped dancing, and he circled me once, twice, our eyes locked, the two of us hidden amidst the arms and legs and undulating torsos. We stood in the silent center of the tempest of all those other bodies, then Reza said to me, "Abji, you have such eyes."

And I, already in love with everything, decided that he was the One. The summation of all of Iran, in the tangible form of a single young man. And a good-looking one, too. Long, thick brown hair he wore tied back in a ponytail. Full beard. Chiseled face. Deep eyes. Hands that looked like they could fell a tree, and hack it and saw it and hew it into a home. He stood before me, the paradigm of Iranian masculinity. Proud. Stoic. Loyal. Good. Honorable. Kind. Capable. In strict control of his emotions, which ran deep, but were concealed and tempered. And since Reza was already devoted, give or take, to his childhood sweetheart, and since he was one of Pouya's closest and oldest friends, having trekked with them since his early adolescence, as well as a sort of adopted son to my Uncle Behrooz, this One was unattainable. Off-limits. Which made him even more desirable. He was the Iran I could never have, the Iran that would never have me.

There'd been only one other boy who affected me like this, a boy I had known since grade school. I knew Kevin was the One when he let me run my toes through the stubble of his hair in the back of Mrs. Harm's second grade classroom. I was seven years old and didn't speak but two words of English, dark-haired, dark eyed, lost in a sea of blond-haired, blued-eyed school kids. Kevin was green-eyed, which shone gold in the sun. Gold skinned. And his hair, an auburn gold. I took off my shoe, removed my sock, and he let me feel the contours of his head with my foot. Right there, between reading groups being called up to the rug, I knew that Kevin was the One.

Kevin was the all-American boy. Played baseball. His dad was a policeman, his mom a homemaker. He knew, from grade school on, that he wanted to be a fireman. "Why a fireman?" I'd ask him later. "You could be anything. Be a senator. Run for president." A fireman. Because he wanted to save people. And take care of his family. Kevin was popular. Everyone admired him. But he was kind, too. Dignified. He kept from the cruelties. He spoke with whomever he pleased, even danced with whomever he pleased at the school dances. Like me. I remember the first time he asked me to dance. It was on the sixth-grade outdoor education trip to Cottontail Ranch, the big dance on the last night, and his favorite song came on. He came up to where I stood, somewhere on the periphery of the dance floor, presumably in the shadows, and asked if I wanted to dance. I cried on his shoulder. I think I may have wiped my nose on his shirt. Inadvertently. But once you've put your toes in someone's hair, all else is permissible.

That same year, Kevin asked me out. At the behest of the popular girls. The Kristies giggled and told him to ask me to go steady. It was the moment I had been waiting for since second grade. I beamed yes. And then I saw, in his eyes, a genuine remorse. "I'm sorry," he said, and he meant it. The Kristies loved it. They roared with laughter. They spoke of it for weeks. They got Ryan to do it next, but this time I was on to them. I wasn't among the girls you'd ask to go steady.

Years later, I got another chance with Kevin at our high school graduation dance. The theme that night was Las Vegas. There were roulette tables, blackjack, even little slot machines. But the dance floor stood empty all night until the song from *Pulp Fiction* came on, where Uma Thurman dances with John Travolta, and I decided *the hell with all of them.* I stepped out of the periphery, out of the shadows, walked out onto the dance floor, right beneath that glittering disco ball, and I danced. The next song, too. And the song after that. By my lonesome, with the rest of them in the peripheries, in the shadows, until someone tapped my shoulder and I turned and there stood Kevin. Tall, proud shoulders, the expanse of his chest just at eye level, blue jeans, white T-shirt, and a cowboy hat on his head. And he asked me to dance. I looked up into his eyes and said, "I'd give anything for you, anything in the world."

"Don't get me wrong," he said. "I like you, and you're real attractive, but you and I, we're just not meant for each other."

The America I could never have, the America that would never have me.

And here I was again, on another dance floor, now locked in Reza's gaze, and he said to me, "Abji, you have such eyes." An echo of Kevin's sentence, *We're just not meant for each other*, summarized by a single word, *abji*. Sister. I like you, don't get me wrong, you have such eyes, but we're just not meant for each other.

There is, of course, no fruit more desirable than the one forbidden. The one out of reach. The unattainable. And it wasn't even mere curiosity that compelled me to want to reach out, to touch, to step closer. It was an urgency to know, to define not just the unknowns of the other, but also the unknowns within myself. But a wall stood between us, between me and Reza. He confessed attraction, then dutifully left me in the middle of that dancing crowd to attend to the broken heart of his childhood sweetheart. I watched him leave. Some other man asked me to dance. And another after that. And the whole time, the whole long night of that party, there was no else in that room save Reza and me.

By dawn, most of the guests had left. Only a few of us remained. Someone filled a water pipe and heated up the coals. Someone brought out some pillows and threw them on the floor. Someone opened a bottle of red wine. Sarab strummed his guitar, and we sang softly. Dylan's "Mr. Tambourine Man." Metallica's "The Unforgiven." Radiohead's "Creep."

Then Pouya and I went to the rooftop of the apartment building to watch the sun rise and the light shift across the landscape. The minarets broadcasted the morning azaan. The song of that prayer echoed across the city. A tint of pink edged the dark sky above the mountains. Below the apartment, in the still shadows, there stood a single man on the edge of a vast, empty field. He had his hands in his pockets. He was waiting. Pacing. The morning azaan continued, and in the silent rooms of homes, people slept, or they prayed. The sky turned gold and orange at the base of a deep blue.

That's when Pouya and I saw her. A woman on the far edge of the field, in the shadow of the mountains, running. She wore a black chador that filled with the wind and blew away from her hair and body as she clutched it with her hands and ran toward the waiting man. The man had his back turned. He did not see her running across that vast field. Then, he gave up. And he started to walk away. She did not call after him, but kept running, faster. And somehow, through some unforeseen connection, some invisible force, he stopped, then turned, and saw her.

He ran to her, and on the edge of that field, the two of them met and embraced. Pouya and I stood watching from the rooftop, in awe, the sole witnesses to this meeting. They embraced for a moment. Then, they kissed. Finally, she pulled away from him, still holding his hands. She stepped back, then turned and ran in the direction from which she came. He watched her leave until she was a distant speck in that endless field. Then he turned and walked down the empty street.

THERE WAS RAMIN, too. Ramin the photographer. He had a mess of thick, black curls and wore Lennon eyeglasses. He was an intellectual. He smoked pipes. He quoted Nietzsche. He was tall and lanky, wore wool cardigans and loafers, slouched when he walked, which gave him an air of aloofness, a young man lost in deep thought. Ramin didn't play music, but he was there most afternoons when the boys and I jammed at Sarab's house. He smoked his pipe, he listened. He watched. When we stopped, he'd delve into some nonchalant existentialism.

One day, Ramin called me at Behrooz's home and asked if I wanted to go to the main bazaar in Tehran. "Sure," I said. "Why not?" A lot of guys called me to ask me out or to invite me to parties. Amir called, too, every few days, just to chat, to see where I was going, who I was seeing, what I had been up to. So when Ramin the photographer called, I thought nothing of it.

"Try to dress normal," he said. "Some parts of downtown are gritty, and it's better not to draw too much attention. I'll be there in an hour."

By then, I had merged Bohemian chic with Islamic hijab seamlessly. Long thrift-store skirts in floral patterns, and in place of the mandatory manteau, I bought fantastically embroidered silk shifts and kaftans handmade by the nomadic tribes, bold colors in a montage of fabrics in dizzying patterns. I wasn't much of a trendsetter on the Tehran scene, but among the girls, who in those days preferred sleeker cuts, clean tailored looks with heels and full makeup, I did manage to stand out. So for the occasion of exploring the gritty parts of downtown Tehran with Ramin the photographer, I pulled on my blue jeans, buttoned up my simple tan linen manteau and covered my hair with the old saffron silk headscarf.

When Ramin showed up at the door, he greeted my uncle and gave him a detailed account of where he wanted to take me and when we'd return. Behrooz told us to have fun. I assumed Ramin was just assuring my uncle of my safety on this sightseeing expedition. While a handful of boys sought my attention in Tehran, Ramin the photographer was just my friend. He certainly hadn't made any overtures of romantic inclinations, not in any fashion I was familiar with, and for all I knew, he was just another one of the boys at Sarab's. Like I was. One of the boys.

To fit in with the artists and musicians in Sarab's home, to be at ease, or rather, to put them at ease, I donned what was considered in that culture as a more masculine identity. Boisterous. Unapologetic. Sexually explicit. I smoked, I argued, I sat and moved at ease with my body. I hid whatever might have been deemed feminine by their standards. It felt like a constant arm-wrestling match. I had to out-boy them. I had to

make them blush. And I liked the role. It was liberating. Not
just in Tehran, where being female imprisoned you to a set of
brutal laws and rigid gender expectations. It was liberating,
period. I liked being *boyish*. I liked sitting in a crowd of young
men and not being identified as a sexual object. It was clear
that I was female, but my mannerisms didn't match their
assumptions of female decorum, so I was a strange, androgy-
nous creature. And that position granted me a liberty I did not
take for granted. None of those boys ever came onto me. Even
in the streets, where the men were notorious for grabbing and
pinching women in passing, I was left alone. I intentionally
walked like a man, boots pounding the pavement with strong
strides and direct, unflinching eye contact. No one ever touched
me. And so when one of my boys, Ramin the photographer,
called to invite me to explore the main bazaar, I never assumed
that he was asking me on a date. I thought it would be an
afternoon of just two buddies, hanging out.

And it was. We hailed a taxi, then ended up downtown.
We talked about capitalism through the passageways of the
main bazaar. We discussed postcolonial theory in Arab Alley
until Ramin noticed a group of shady men eyeing us, grabbed
my elbow, and hurried his pace, not interrupting his own
soliloquy on the debilitating role of American imperialism in
the economic progress of third world nations. We talked in
hushed voices about the failure of the 1979 Revolution in an
old coffee shop that used to house the communists, the artists, and the general dissidents during the reign of the Shah.
We stood in front of the central mosque debating the role of
religion in the enslavement of the proletariat.

He took me to the Imam Zadeh, the burial site of one of the descendants of the prophet Muhammed, where we finally stopped talking and arguing because we were separated into two lines, one for men and one for women. I entered a room to find a shrine beneath the tepid glow of halogen lights, where a crowd of women sat praying and weeping, pleading for miracles. Afterward, Ramin invited me to a famous Turkish coffee shop, where the proprietor was renowned for his ability to read your future in the grounds left behind in the cup, but he only did so for select patrons whom he trusted, because the Islamic theocracy had outlawed the reading of coffee grounds.

Ramin begged the man to ignore the censorship that silenced his art of ground reading, to trust us as we were his comrades in struggle, to please read our future in the bottom of our cups, until the man finally acquiesced. It was a wonderful and exhausting afternoon. And the only intimate moment between us was when Ramin and I were walking past the spice vendors and Ramin said something that made me stop and laugh out loud. He turned in a panic and placed his entire hand over my mouth to silence me. "You can't do that!" he whispered, close to my face, his hand still over my mouth. He let go of me, looked around us quickly, then turned and walked, motioning for me to follow.

"Do what?" I asked, hurrying along.

"Laugh. Out loud. In public."

"Why?"

"Don't you know? It is against the law. A woman should not be heard in public. Not even the sound of her shoes. Didn't you see all those people staring at you?"

I didn't. I hadn't noticed anybody staring at me. Why should I have? I was only laughing. Engaged in a dialogue. Not cognizant of my gender, and the rules ascribed to that. I paid heed to all the other rules in public now. Cover your body, cover your hair. No red bikini in front of strangers, no swimming in the open, blue seas. No display of desire. No walking unchaperoned by a male kin, alone in the brilliant light of morning. Or at dusk. Certainly never at night. No shaking the hands of the merchant who sold you soap at a bargain price. No sockless ankles. No sitting beside epileptic coal sellers on the street. No riding bicycles, no public singing. Or dancing. But laughter?

This was fodder for intellectual debate, so I started in on Ramin, on the nonsense of a woman not being allowed to laugh out loud and not only his own complacency, but his active participation in its enforcement, but Ramin was clearly nervous, insisting that we were in danger, and that particular discourse would have to wait.

BY THE END of that August in 2001, Tehran was my scene. I spent the mornings do-gooding for the downtrodden, the afternoons jamming with my boys, the evenings dancing at secret parties or strolling through art galleries or smoking hookah at local chai khanehs with a group of friends. Just when the city became too much, Uncle Behrooz would organize a trekking trip, and we'd pack our gear and set out into Iran's wilderness, climbing mountains by day, singing beside campfires beneath the star-littered skies at night.

In between, whenever inspiration struck, I sat down and wrote poetry. The days were hot, languid, hazy, and complete. I felt a wholeness I had never felt before. I was beautiful, desirable, talented. I was compassionate. I was interesting. The world, my oyster, and I, its pearl. Everything was as it should be. America would wait for me and Justin had become a distant memory. The prognosis of a defective heart was forgotten, and my father's death a reminder to indulge in life, a license to be.

On the last Thursday of that August in 2001, after a particularly hot week, Pouya, Javid, and I received an invitation to a weekend fete at a seaside condo in a gated community near Feraydoon Kenar, the tiny village beside the Caspian where a certain golden fisherman lived.

On the long drive to the seashore, I mentioned to Javid that since we were so close to Feraydoon Kenar, I wanted to visit that quaint fishing village again, just to hire out a boat and sit in the middle of the sea. Neither he nor Pouya knew anything about the golden fisherman, so Javid agreed to drive me over the following morning. By the time we arrived at the gated community, it was already dark and we walked in through the door dancing, and danced well into the early hours of the morning, but the whole of that night all I could think about was my close proximity to him, the golden fisherman, and his red boat and his blue sea.

Bright and early the next day, Javid drove us along that stretch of flat highway between the two seaside villages, less than ten kilometers, until we reached the gravel road that ended in the sand. He parked near the small general market on the beach, and I jumped out of the car to scan the shoreline.

No golden fisherman in sight.

Just Ahmad, mending a net. Javid greeted Ahmad warmly, the two of them buddies now. Javid told Ahmad I needed to sit in the middle of the sea. Ahmad put away the net, pushed his boat into the water while Javid removed his shoes and waded into the waves.

I suppose I assumed the golden fisherman a permanent feature of that seashore, like the market and the birds and the sea itself. The idea that he might not be there never even crossed my mind. Javid waited in the boat for me, and since I couldn't argue why this fisherman was not the right fisherman for the job, I took off my shoes and reluctantly boarded Ahmad's boat. Ahmad started the motor.

In the middle of the sea, we sat for a spell in silence, bobbing in the waves. After what Javid felt was a sufficient amount of time for musing, he asked if I was ready to leave. And I, glum beneath the morning sun, said, "Yeah. I'm done. Let's go."

Back on shore, Javid, particular about the cleanliness of his car, was directed by Ahmad to a waterspout behind the small general market where we could rinse the sand from our feet. I trudged behind him, dejected. And lo and behold, there stood the golden fisherman, leaning against the wall, cigarette in hand, exhaling smoke, dreamy-eyed. He turned and saw me standing behind Javid. But he couldn't let on his emotions, because even though the police weren't there, or the angry village women, the hulking body of Javid was. And Javid was my guardian, and I was a single girl, and he was a fisherman.

The existing taboos in Iran are culturally specific, but there are some universal ones, too. And one of these universal taboos is that a woman from a certain socioeconomic class cannot give herself to a man beneath her class. I learned this from the Afghan refugees who were all over Tehran that summer. All young men fleeing the Taliban, leaving in droves, by foot, running across the mountains, across the borders, many of whom found themselves in Tehran, where work was plentiful. And what beautiful young men they were. I'm not sure what elegant sequence of genomes came together, what history of rape and war and conquest led to this, but these boys were blond and tan-skinned, tall and light eyed, with cheekbones to die for. I'd see them walking in the streets and, as a young woman of a certain class, was not allowed to notice their beauty. But holy mess if I could keep my eyes off them. I asked the few girlfriends I had if they noticed this mass of Dolce and Gabbana models walking around, or was I hallucinating, and the girls denied that they noticed, and if they had, they denied that there was even a modicum of desirability in these men. Another note on taboo, it is hard to transcend. It pushes things deep into the unconscious mind, forces us to hide parts of ourselves, to mask the truths of our wanting for fear of repercussions. For aeons, men have etched these rules into stone tablets, exiled and maimed trespassers, killed the ones who dared. Naturally, it was a safer bet to deny any desire that lay beyond these sanctioned borders. So, the Afghan refugees were off-limits, and my fisherman, too. And the golden fisherman knew this, knew that he was a fisherman and that I was an educated young woman from a respectable family of the hardworking middle class, and woe be the day we tipped this fine balance. So he greeted Javid and nodded a nonchalant greeting in my direction, then joined Javid at the spout while my cousin rinsed his sandy feet.

Two months had passed between our first meeting and this moment. Two months of poetry written about that moment of grace between us, that ineffable and divine longing. In the span of that time, he had become a metaphor, but now, suddenly, he stood before me in flesh and form. And I stood frozen to the spot. I couldn't find the tongue to address him. I couldn't bring myself to look into his eyes. Javid rinsed his feet and the golden fisherman sat down on a log near the waterspout, looking out to sea, his back to Javid, while the two chatted. Javid sat down beside him, meticulously dusted off his toes, then rose, bade him farewell, and started for the car when he remembered me.

"Could you rinse your feet before you get in my car?" he asked.

Javid left me standing there alone beside the waterspout. I didn't have much to work with, but I did have a keen aptitude for seduction and an uncanny resourcefulness. At my disposal, one waterspout, two sandy feet with red-painted toenails, and a little less than ten minutes. If the female form is veiled, hidden for fear that every aspect of it gleams with temptation inspired by the devil, imagine, then, the power of red-painted toenails, the delicate arch of the foot, the ankle. There he sat, his beautiful straight back, the taut muscles beneath his shirt, the fine, sinewy neck, the soft golden down of his skin, those hairs raised by my proximity, standing erect to feel the minute shift of air currents caused by the motion of my body in the approximation of his. Only these small hairs attested to his awareness of my presence, giving away our secret. The rest of him sat motionless, feigning disinterest, his back turned to where I stood beside the waterspout, but at a slight angle, so that he could still watch me from the corner of his eyes.

I walked to the waterspout. I lifted the hem of my skirt slightly, then extended my foot. I turned the water on, a gentle trickle, which hit the top of my foot and ran in small rivulets down to the spaces between my toes, leaving the skin washed of its sand a stark contrast to the dust of the rest. I turned my foot, pointed my toes to extenuate the arch, then lifted the hem of my skirt just a bit higher, above my ankle bone, and turned the water to a steadier, harder stream. The cold jet of it hit my skin with more force, sending droplets of water dazzling into the sunlight. I lifted my skirt higher still, to my shin, just below the naked curve of my calf.

Here, both his attention and mine were so acutely focused on this singular visceral experience, the washing of my feet, that we lost that distinction between our separate bodies. Through that transcendent annihilation of self for want of the other, he became me, felt the possession of my foot, and I became him, felt his wanting, and that foot became an extension of this shared body. I slowed the water back to a trickle. I shut it off. I rested my foot on the spout and dried my toes slowly with the hem of my skirt.

One foot down, one foot to go.

We had only this left, the duration of time it would take for me to wash my other foot, before an indeterminable distance separated us again. He spoke, quietly, his back to me.

He brought his cigarette to his mouth to hide the motion of his lips, and he said, "Come back tomorrow. Without your cousin."

"How?" I asked.

The rest of the whole wide world saw only a young woman washing her feet at a waterspout. The rest of the whole wide world saw a young man near that spout, smoking a cigarette, his back turned, looking out to sea. The world saw these two strangers, disconnected from each other, engaged in their own experiences, just passing. The world did not see the magical stardust of the universe that burned between them.

"Hire a cab," he said. "Come early in the morning, when the beach is still empty."

I washed my other foot. Slowly.

"I'm afraid," I said.

Javid honked the horn. Intrusive, the sound blasted the delicate intimacy, the gentle exchange of whispers between us. Whispers are a form of touch, too. When touch is forbidden, the distance between two bodies unreachable, a whisper feels like the caress of fingertips down the soft skin of the neck.

I dried my foot.

He stood up, took a step farther away from me and threw the spent cigarette butt into the sand. "Will you come?" he asked, without turning to look at me. Javid honked again.

"Yes," I said.

I walked to the car. I didn't look back. I don't know where he went after that. Javid drove us back to the gated community, but I wanted nothing to do with the crowd at that party.

I told Javid to go inside without me, that I intended to go for a walk, alone.

I left the gated community and walked along the two-lane highway that stretched lazily between those slow, sun-drenched, humid villages. I walked past a lagoon with egrets and turtles, past rice paddies full of women in colorful scarves tending to the crop, until I reached a field of tall grass turning blond in the sun. I walked into that open field until I came to a wall. An enclosure, the perimeter small enough that I walked around the whole thing within a minute. Four walls, and no roof. In the middle of a field. A garden? The wall was short enough for me to climb. I hoisted myself up and sat on top, my heart racing, wondering what in this field of tall, rolling grass needed to be walled in. In that small enclosed space there was more tall grass and, in its midst, a single old gnarled fruit tree. Nothing more. No muted, ravenous beast. No bones. No fantastic flowers or gurgling fountains or piles of gold. Just a single old tree.

For some reason, perhaps the fact that it was enclosed, I felt an urgency to trespass. Why, in all this open space, wall in something so insignificant? Would the ground of that enclosed space give way beneath my feet? Did a nest of snakes, entire generations born there, inbred, evolved separate of the snakes in the vicinity, wait hidden in that grass? I didn't stop to figure out the meaning of this seemingly forgotten garden in the middle of an empty field. Something about it felt forbidden, and that forbiddance, in and of itself, beckoned its own transgression with a powerful draw. I jumped down into that walled space.

The earth did give, a bit, beneath me. The world sounded with the buzz, the hum, the chatter, the singing of ten thousand living things. I walked to the tree with slow, hesitant steps. I don't know how much time passed as I stood there, but somewhere in that indeterminable period, I understood that this wasn't a place for me. I walked across the garden to the wall opposite of the first one I scaled, climbed up and jumped back into the open field. Above me, an unchanged, unseeing blue sky.

We spent the afternoon by the beach. There was barbeque and beer and volleyball. By evening, I was so on edge, that everything surrounding me felt like an intrusion, an obstacle between me and my golden fisherman. I retired to a quiet room, shunned the society of my friends, to wait out the night. I sat there alone and listened to the conversations that carried above the music. That's when I noticed a certain change in the pitch of the female voices when they addressed the guys at the party. An octave higher. Almost childlike. Even their laughter indicated the presence of an eligible man, modified to appease, to attract, to assure him of his power, his desirability. In the bazaar, a woman was not allowed to laugh out loud. In public, she was not to be heard, but even here, among friends, how free was she to express herself?

Just then, as I recalled that moment when Ramin the photographer placed his entire hand over my mouth to silence me, a few girls walked into the room and asked why I wasn't joining the festivities. And so I launched into a speech about the liberation of our sisters from the systematic dehumanization enacted upon us by the patriarchy. It was a talk of the inspirational variety, complete with fist pounding the air, voice amplified by truth, a golden light shining upon me as I pontificated on our enslavement as women. Soon, the girls all sat around me in that room while the boys waited pensively in the living room, wondering what sort of secret female rite drew all the girls away from the party.

"Why change your voices?" I demanded. "Why soften it each time you speak to a man? Why swallow your dissensions to your fathers, your brothers, your boyfriends?" The girls murmured their approval. We sat in that room, our oppressors separated from us by a wall. "The time is nigh," I proclaimed. "We cannot allow them to imprison us with their expectations, their laws, their rules. We cannot, for fear of our reputations, be kept calm and quiet and still!" Louder approval. I stood amongst those girls, my eyes gazing at the future that waited past our struggle, where we'd freely dance naked in some forest, with spears in our hands and garlands of daisies in our hair. "Let us strip ourselves of the yoke they have put upon us! Let us renounce the sanctity of the hymen! Let them know that we will no longer be beholden to this piece of skin!"

And that's when I lost them.

Just like that. The rapture ended, the band stopped the march, the golden light flickered off, and they looked at me in shocked, dead silence. "Are you saying that virginity is not important?" a girl named Farah asked, eyes welling with tears.

"No! No, it is not important. We are more than this! I am more than this! My worth is not tied to what happens or does not happen between my legs!"

I might as well have turned into a giant lizard in that moment, the way they looked at me. Farah actually broke into tears. Real, flowing tears. She ran out of that room to the boys sitting in the other room, sobbing, heaving, pleading for them to give her protection from my heresy. She had had her eye on Javid for months now, and this was a magnificent political move on her behalf, a strategy that immediately secured her place as a marriage-worthy chaste girl, attacked for her righteousness by the corrupting propaganda of the slut from Los Angeles. Javid actually came into the room, now empty of all my constituents, who abandoned the cause and returned to party with the boys, and he gave me some kind cousinly advice about being more discreet with my "ideas." Then he returned to the party, too.

Hurt that I had been forsaken, that the revolution had been aborted before it even had a chance to breathe, I turned my thoughts to the following morning. What was I to wear? Bikini beneath the burqa? No one wears a burqa in Iran, but I couldn't resist the alliteration, purple prose writer that I am. No. No bikini. A bikini would mean that I would swim with him. No swimming with him. A dress, instead. A blue silk dress with little white flowers. I'd remove the manteau once we reached the open sea and stand before his male gaze, coyly innocent in a blue silk dress.

I awoke the next morning and explained to Javid my intentions to hire a boat and told him I'd return that afternoon. I called a cab. We drove past the sleepy lagoons and the pastoral scene of women bent over rice paddies, then turned onto the gravel road and stopped before the sand. I paid the cab driver and told him to return at half past the noon azaan, and to wait for me, should I be late, that I'd pay him for his time. The cab driver bid me farewell and drove away.

What in G.d's good name was I doing there, on that empty beach, secretly meeting a fisherman in the Islamic Republic of Iran?

But that thought never crossed my mind. In that moment, in the actual moment, I believed fully in the magic of things. In destiny. In the power of a good narrative lived. I ignored danger, I refused to write fear into my story. Only desire. Only forbiddance, which heightened that desire. The golden fisherman was a creation of mine. I, myself, was a creation of mine. The very beach, the seagulls, everything, parts of a story I intended.

He stood by the water, dazzling in the sunlight. When he pushed the boat into the sea, I climbed in and sat at the front, looking out to the horizon. We did not speak a word to each other. He sat behind me. I felt him watching my back. The wind caught in the silk headscarf I wore, then blew my hair wild as we escaped from that shore. When we were far enough not to be seen, he shut off the motor.

Silence.

Save the birds. And the deafening lull of that tremendous body of water, beneath which an entire universe glimmered in secret darkness. The boat rocked in the gentle waves. I finally turned to look at him, knowing that to look at him might obliterate me and him and law and time and all else I knew. He sat there, in the soft morning light, watching me.

"Swim with me," he said, finally.

"I can't. I didn't wear a bathing suit."

"No matter," he said. He stood up, then stripped off his white T-shirt. What can I say? Really, we don't pay enough homage to the male physique. He might have been some fashion model, standing in that red boat with all that blue surrounding him. Some beautiful young man in the glossy pages of a magazine, with his sinewy golden arms and his lean body and the taut of his belly, the build of a man who labors with his body. He stood there and had I an easel and some oil paints, I'd have painted a portrait of his utterly devastating perfection.

"Swim with me," he said, again.

"I can't. I decided I wouldn't. It wouldn't be right. Anyway, all I have on is a dress. It's best I don't."

"Swim in your dress."

How could I tell him I wore that dress as a way of placing a hard and fast rule for myself? I had decided not to swim with him, to just sit in the boat and look pretty. To be in the middle of the sea alone with him was overwhelming enough. Too much unknown. To sit in the midst of that existential immensity usurped all the courage I had, but to swim in it with this man? The touch of that water and his hands just might lead to the spontaneous dissipation of my whole body. No. Cannot. Will not.

Okay, fine.

I unbuttoned my manteau, slipped it off and stood there, bared shoulders, bared arms, the wind blowing the silk of my dress against my body. I looked him straight in the eyes, then turned and dove into the water. And he dove in right after me.

It occurred to me, under that water, that we had just crossed some threshold. Our act, if witnessed, would certainly bring upon us the vengeance of any Islamic judge. But here, in the blind sea, beneath a blind sky, all of that could be ignored, momentarily forgotten, and we could now give ourselves, with complete abandon, to our desire. Beneath the surface, we sought each other's hands. Just that. The hands, seeking one another. I tired and swam to hold onto the side of the boat. He followed me, put his hands on either side of mine.

"Tired?" he whispered into my ear.

I nodded yes.

"Let's get into the boat and rest."

I lay on a bench beneath the warm sun, the wet silk of my dress pasted against my skin. He opened a couple cans of soda and offered me one. "You will return to Los Angeles," he said.

"Yes."

"And I'll stay here. Forever."

"Do you want to leave?"

"You will forget me," he said.

"I won't. I can't."

"Stay with me, then," he said.

"How?"

"Marry me. Live here with me. As my wife."

He moved closer to me, knelt beside the bench where I lay. He touched me. His lips found mine. We kissed, deeply. After, he pulled away from me, threw his head back, and let out a deep moan. He stood up, walked to the front of the boat. Looked out to sea. I watched him, and he stood somewhere outside of time. He stands there still, eternal, and from that place, perhaps, he looks back at me. Then, he turned and dove into the water.

He stayed beneath the surface for a long while. I watched for him, anxiously. When he shot out of that water, he took in a breath that swallowed the whole world. With that breath, he swallowed me, too. I entered him and felt the pleasure of his lungs filling with air. I felt the pleasure of his body. The strength of it. Its virility. I felt him as though I were that man, in that body, in that water, satiated by a woman, calmed by the sea. And I felt something else, too. Something in his gaze. The dazzle of that immense mystery between us had dimmed a bit. A distance appeared, instead. A particular loneliness. Just then, the azaan arose from the speakers of the mosques, the prayer that signaled noon. My cab would arrive in half an hour.

"I have to go soon," I said.

"Don't go."

"I have to."

"Then come back again."

"I can't."

"To marry me?"

"I can't."

"Why?"

"I can't."

To read love into this story would be an error. This is not a love story. Love is another beast altogether. This story is about longing, about desire, about forbiddance, and how forbiddance, in and of itself, beckons its own transgression with a powerful draw. And once I had scaled the wall and stood in that forbidden place, I knew, with certainty and without explanation, that it wasn't a place for me. The perimeter, too small. The sky above, endless. Unenclosed. And to accept those walls, to ignore the great expanse of experience beyond them . . . I couldn't. Even if it meant denying that golden man and the fantasy of being a fisherman's wife and cooking stews on the hearth of a small picturesque stone hut with a thatched roof and primitive furniture and a tin can full of wildflowers on a wooden table with a hand-stitched linen tablecloth, the truth of the matter was, to accept this story, I would have to forgo all other potential narratives that I sensed life held for me.

A half hour left before the cab arrived. The noon azaan echoed from the minarets of the mosque. The song carried out to sea. On shore, a host of witnesses waited for our return. All we had left were these brief moments. And in them a regret, that growing distance, the heaviness of goodbye. We spent that last half hour stretching time so that, forever, in both our minds, we sit in an embrace in a little red boat in the middle of a blue sea with no future and no past.

He held my hand as I stepped out of his boat for the last time. A group of men stood by the market. Village men. They saw me take hold of his hand, saw that my shoulder grazed his chest when I lost my footing, saw that he placed an arm around my waist to steady me. I walked ahead of him, to the waiting cab, where he opened the car door. I got in, quietly. He shut the door without a word. As the cab drove slowly down the gravel road away from the sea, I looked out of the rear window and saw him standing there, hands in his pockets.

He raised one in goodbye. I rolled down the window and leaned out fully, my hair blowing wildly from beneath my veil.

He watched after me until the taxi turned the bend. Then, he must have turned to face the group of men who stood witness to this ending.

WHEN I RETURNED to Tehran from the Caspian Sea, Ramin the photographer invited me over to his apartment. "You said you make good Mexican food," he said. "We can search for the ingredients at a bazaar near my place and cook them in my kitchen."

Lavash for tortillas, kidney beans for pinto, enough cumin to mask the difference, we made our way through the bazaar talking and I, careful of laughter, selected ripe tomatoes, chili peppers, yellow onions. In his apartment, the walls were lined with shelves, the shelves full of books, the floor full of books, the coffee table stacked with books, the couch worn. He put on a Leonard Cohen record and the smooth bass of Cohen's voice filled the home. I admonished him for the black thing he called a pot as we washed and chopped the produce. He told me about his father, who was ill for some time then died, leaving him all alone. He showed me framed photographs of his relatives.

Ramin the photographer came from a long line of intellectuals who were either dead, exiled, or forced to escape the country. The only relatives he had in Tehran were his distant cousins and an elderly uncle, near blind. He told me about his formidable lineage as he selected a pipe from a collection on his desk, opened the pouch of tobacco he carried in his breast pocket, and filled the bowl. In the quiet street outside, a peddler passed, singing about the coal he sold. And the sunlight filtered into that room, and a breeze came in through the open window and that peddler's song carried in, too, and the smoke of Ramin's pipe rose into the air, swirled in the eddies of the wind, and I stood barefoot on a tattered rug, and the scent of chili and cumin and onion filled the room, while Cohen swooned, *You live your life as if it's real*, and I allowed myself to slip right into that masterpiece, the perfection of that afternoon, when I was beautiful and the world was beautiful and life stretched herself wide and inviting before me.

"Do you want to hear a story?" I asked Ramin.

He looked at me through the smoke of his pipe, in the haze of the sunlight. "A story?"

"About a girl and her golden fisherman."

"Sure."

So I told Ramin the photographer the story, that once upon a time from a land far away, a girl returned home, and she came to a shore and found a red boat, and a fisherman who shone gold, and that fisherman took her into the middle of the blue sea, and saw her naked wrist and then touched her soul. I told him how she witnessed divinity in the desire of his eyes. I told him of her return to that seashore. I told Ramin the photographer about the waterspout, the arch of the foot, the trickle of water, the glimpse of the calves, the whispered conversation. I told him how the next morning she stepped into the golden fisherman's boat and, in the middle of the sea, swam with him, and the moment he asked her to be his wife.

And then, I told Ramin the photographer how the golden fisherman kissed that girl, and how he tasted in her mouth. And later, how he had stood at the edge of his boat, then jumped into the sea, surfaced, then swallowed her and the whole world, too, and how, after, she felt the loss of something. A fading in the sunlight.

Ramin listened with rapt attention. When I finished the story, he looked at me for a while, in silence, then asked, "And this happened in Feraydoon Kenar?"

"Yes."

"What was the fisherman's name? His real name?"

"I don't know . . . I don't know. Perhaps he told me. Certainly, he must have told me, but he was the golden fisherman. That was his name. What other name did he need?"

Ramin looked at me for a while longer, without speaking. He had finished his pipe. The beans simmered on the stove in the kitchen, the street outside silent as the neighborhood rested in the hours of the afternoon. The dust motes hung suspended in the rays of sunlight that came into the room and spilled across my bare legs on the couch. Ramin put his pipe on the coffee table, stood up and said, "I'll be right back." Then he went into his bedroom.

I thought about my golden fisherman. About how I couldn't remember his name. Maybe I hadn't acknowledged the golden fisherman's humanity? Maybe I had ascribed him the role of object so that, like the American tourist that I was, I could have the experience, as though experience, too, was like the tchotchke you bought from a local artisan in an open-air market. Maybe. But my intentions were honest, weren't they?

I felt, and he felt, too, an unbearable gulf, a question, a void, a *something* that needed to be filled by knowledge. Our hands, our lips, our bodies answered. The answer now existed. Surely, we could have spent a lifetime building on that answer. But I couldn't really marry a fisherman. And he must have known, too, known that to marry me, to spend a lifetime answering that question would not have worked.

Just then, Ramin the photographer came back into the living room. He was wearing a white poet's shirt, unbuttoned, and nothing else.

"What are you doing?" I asked.

"What do you mean?"

"What are you doing?"

"Isn't this what you want?"

He walked over to the couch. I leaned back into the cushions, hoped for the cushions to hide me, far away from him, from his nakedness, from the look in his eyes.

"What do I want?" I asked.

"This," and he leaned down toward me, his hands on either side of me on the cushions.

"From you? We're friends!"

"But you told me that story . . ."

"I told you a story!"

"You are in my home, cooking for me . . ." He stood back up, naked, his arms open, in question, in accusation.

"We're friends!" I cried.

He turned, angry, retreated to the bedroom, returned clothed fully in a pair of jeans, his shirt buttoned. "You are in my home," he said. "Alone." He sat on the couch beside me, his shaking hand reached for the pipe, then filled it with tobacco again. "You told me that story. What do you think I would think?"

"That I'm in your home, telling you a story!"

"I'm sorry. I misunderstood."

"I didn't even know . . ."

He looked at me, incredulous. Inhaled smoke. Looked away from me. "The way you dance," he said. "You know I watch you. The way you talk, like you're open . . . you know, free . . . about these things. And all the times I've come to your uncle's home to take you out. And, now, you're here, alone, in my home, with your bare legs in that dress, telling me stories about what you did with a fisherman? What did you think I would think?"

I didn't answer. He kept his eyes away from me.

"I think the beans are ready," I said, finally. "But I have to go. Now. Could you get me a cab?"

When the cab honked in the street outside a few minutes later, he held open the door to his home. "It's best if you leave alone," he told me. "I don't want my neighbors to see us together and think things."

That night at a party at Sarab's house, I performed my poetry while the boys improvised on their instruments. I knew that Ramin the photographer was there, somewhere, watching. We had greeted one another earlier like nothing had happened. He had his camera that night, and he was taking pictures. Some girl in a short skirt, with short hair and red lips, seemed to have his attention, at least the focus of his lens, anyway. The whole of the night, he did not address me.

A famous painter was there, a middle-aged woman who was well known and sold her work in galleries throughout Europe. After our performance, she called me over, in the dark of that home. She sat, regal on the couch, smoking a cigarette. "Sit with me," she said. I had been told of who she was, and those who told me spoke with reverence. She studied me for a while in the dim light.

"I watched you dancing earlier," she told me. "You have a beautiful body." She took a drag on her cigarette, blew out the smoke, leaned in closer. "You move like poetry. And are you a poet?"

"I would like to be."

She placed her hand on my thigh and said, "You cannot choose to be a poet. You are either born one or you are not."

Hours after midnight on our drive home, Pouya and I decided to stop for juice from one of the stands that was open all night on the main avenue. There weren't many people on the street in the early hours of that morning. Just the street sweepers in their ill-fitting, government-issued, orange jumpsuits holding their wooden brooms. They stood, an army of those haggard men, beneath the strung lightbulbs up and down the street, in the flurry of sycamore leaves, and they swept and they swept and they swept.

In front of the juice stand, in the light of its neon sign, stood three foreigners and a couple Iranian men, all in finely tailored suits, heavy watches on their wrists, holding their cups of juice, rocking on their heels, talking with voices booming. They laughed with the air of assured men. Powerful men. Men who made secret and lucrative deals. The foreigners spoke

German. The Iranian men responded in German. They must have had ties to the government. Everyone who had money in Iran, who made lucrative deals, had ties to the government. Behind the men, at a distance, there stood an old man. A street sweeper in his loose, orange jumpsuit. He leaned on his broom, barely standing.

I walked past the businessmen, aware that they were watching me. Smelling me. I felt their attention, felt it in my body. An animal alertness, a strange surge of adrenaline. A girl, dressed so oddly, at this hour, alone on the street. I walked up to the old street sweeper and said, "Father, it is so late, what are you doing on the street, working at this hour?"

"Fire," he mumbled, without seeing me. "Fire fell from the skies. Burned up the village. And they died, one by one. They died." He was one of the refugees from Afghanistan, I could tell from his accent.

"Who? Who died, father?" He stopped and he looked at me, trying to focus on my face. He had been crying. That old man, on the street, in the middle of a cold, almost autumn night. He held his broom, barely able to stand, and he had been crying.

"Who died?" I asked again.

"My children," he said. "My children died. Before the spring."

And something in me broke. Like shattered glass, like fragmented concrete, and I felt a crushing weight, a crumbling of my soul, a thunderous fall, the shower of dust and debris, and rock and silt. Behind me, I could hear the businessmen talking, laughing, assured, powerful. Watching me. Assuming.

Surely. Assuming that since it was night, and I stood alone, dressed so oddly in such bold colors, with the scent of sweat on my body, that surely I was the sort of girl who visited young men alone in their apartments, stood bare-legged on tattered rugs in the light of the afternoon, and told stories about nameless fishermen and desire. So I turned, and I walked up to those businessmen, with the strut they expected of me, and stood real close to the tallest German among them, the one who thrust his chest out more than the others, the one who had the hungriest eyes, and I looked at him and asked, "Do you have money?"

And they laughed, those men, laughed the laugh of men who assume the world to be lucrative, to bend and give to their needs. And the German replied, "How much do you need?"

And I leaned into him and said, "Show me your generosity."

And the men looked at one another, like wolves, maybe, signaling something unspoken amongst themselves, and the German smiled and reached into his pocket, took out a fold of bills and made a show to count out several, before he handed it to me. "Is that enough for you to show me your generosity?" he asked.

"Of course," I said. I smiled, licked my lips, like a wolf, maybe. Then I turned and walked away, to where the old man stood sweeping, and I took his arm and placed the money in his hand, closed his fingers around the bills and said, "Go home, father, go get some rest."

I could feel the men watching me. I had breached our contract. The German men looked angry, but the glares of the Iranian men were burning. I had humiliated them, certainly, before their guests. I, an Iranian girl, should have known my part on that night, alone, in the street. I walked past them, without a word, to where Pouya waited for me in the car. We drove home. To sleep.

IN THE LATE afternoon of a September day, I lay in my bed naked, damp with sweat, the sheets crumpled around me as I watched the curtains dance, impregnated by the breeze. The scent of the city had changed. It carried a smokiness to it now, and the musk of fallen leaves. The afternoons were still hot, but the evenings held the chill of the impending autumn. Blackbirds called to one another from the roof of the mosque outside my window.

Then, a stillness, and in that moment of their silence, the phone rang.

Behrooz called my name from the living room. "It's your mother," he said.

I put on a T-shirt, pulled on my jeans. I walked out of my room and Behrooz held out the phone to me without looking at me. He was searching for the remote control to the TV with an urgency, a panic I had never seen in him.

"Mom?"

"Are you watching the TV?" she asked.

"Why?"

"We are being attacked."

"What?"

"Turn on the TV. New York is under attack."

"What?"

Behrooz turned on the TV. On the rooftops of apartment buildings all across Tehran were hidden satellites. Inside homes all across the city, the people were secretly watching television channels outlawed by the Islamic regime. And we watched, too. We watched, stunned, among the millions of others who watched, stunned. There stood the Twin Towers, one already crumbling down to dust. We watched in silence at what looked like blackbirds at first, falling from the buildings.

"Those are people," my mother wept into the phone. "Those are people. Jumping."

THE CITY WAS congested with traffic, the street below our apartment flooded by the devout pouring out of the mosque. Festival lights strung from telephone poles shone brightly to mark the birthday of another imam. A strange, frenzied dread, an awful uncertainty, hung heavy in the air. The smog, the heavy exhaust of the cars, the heat, the scents of the city, human sweat, fermenting fruit, fallen leaves, smoke, the sudden shock of the perfume of tuberose the street children sold at traffic stops, the horns, the screeches, the cacophony of human voices, the lights, everything felt like an assault. I waited for a late taxi with Sarab, Shervin, Amir, Sanam, and Pouya. We were leaving Tehran for the city of Yazd. The rest of our party was to meet us down at the train station.

Amir had planned this trip. A group of ten of us would go to the city of Yazd by train, then hire a car to drive us through the empty surrounding desert in search of an ancient Zoroastrian temple named Chak Chak. Our arrival at that temple would fall on the night of the Autumn Equinox, when the Zoroastrians celebrated the harvest and a deity named Mehr, who originally represented the covenant of friendship and purification by fire but, over time, would come to be known as the king of warfare.

More than a week had passed since the fall of the Twin Towers in New York City. America had already named her enemies, Iran among them, and scheduled a preemptive strike on Afghanistan. The night before our trip, we watched the president of the United States on television. "Either you are with us, or you are with the terrorists," he had said.

Amir suggested that we visit the ancient Zoroastrian fire temple, lost in a desert, on the night consecrated by the deity of the covenant of friendship, who then became the deity of warfare, to wait out this turn history was about to take.

"There is no way we'll make that train," Amir said.

"We are already on that train," I said. "We have arrived at the temple, we have lived our whole lives, grown old, and rotted in our graves. We are bones. We are the dust of the universe, waiting to be conceived."

I was on edge, belligerent with anxiety. The apprehension in the air was stifling. The approach of the American planes, the impending bombs. The American news channels I watched obsessively showed supposed crowds of people celebrating the September 11 attacks in Tehran's streets. But when I walked along those same streets, there were no traces of celebratory crowds. What I did see was an alarming disconnect between events as they happened, and how they were spun into a new and terrifying narrative in the global media. Everything felt strangely dislodged from reality. All of it, the politics, the theater of powerful men, seemed a sham. But beyond it, beyond all the sound and the fury, beyond the gnashing of teeth and pounding of chests, there was something like a faint glimmer of light, something that begged to be seen, to be called into being.

Late, the taxi crawled painfully through the traffic. The taxi driver said, "You will never make that train."

"We are on that train already," I replied. "And already born and already rotting in our graves. All this at once, so don't worry."

At the station, we jumped out of the car and ran. The train whistled, it moaned and clattered, and the wheels ached and turned and the train began to pull away from the platform. We ran harder, our backpacks heavy. We grabbed hold of the hand rails, hoisted ourselves, each one in turn, on board. All ten of us, somehow, from all corners of the city, out of breath, flushed, managed to make that train. It carried us out of the city and into a desert, through a dark, empty night.

After the American president's address on the television, Ramin the photographer called me. I told him I was leaving Tehran for a couple of nights to see Yazd. Then I said, "I think I need to return to Los Angeles soon after that."

"You need to forgive me," he said.

"I don't know how we can be friends now," I said.

"I don't want to be your friend," he said.

"We can't be anything else."

"On your way to Yazd, look out of the train window at midnight and think about me."

"What should I look for?"

"Nothing."

At midnight, I left our cabin. The tight hall was full of passengers standing by the open windows, smoking. They stood by the windows with the pretense of their cigarettes, and flirted with strangers in whispers and allowed themselves to fall in love. I found an empty window. I thought about Ramin. I looked out into the darkness and saw an endless nothing.

The town of Yazd was a dream made out of sand. Beautiful ancient buildings the same color as the earth, save the gold on the gilded domes of the mosques. Quiet, peaceful, it rose out of the ground as though nature intended the buildings, the alleyways, the domes and walls. When we arrived, the town was still asleep. We walked through the streets searching for a cab just as the azaan sounded from the minarets, calling the Muslims to prayer.

Yazd is a city populated by Zoroastrians. Though this religious group is a minority in Iran, their numbers are concentrated in this city. In the old days, the Zoroastrians took their dead to the top of a mountain, to a circular, walled enclosure that had no roof. They lay their dead beneath the naked skies on stone slabs, where the vultures cleaned the bones, and the sun bleached those clean bones dry. The Tower of Silence still stands in Yazd, at the top of a mountain. But the dead are buried in the foothills now, in neat rows beneath green grass watered by sprinkler systems.

We were sober that morning. Quiet. The gravity of it all felt a bit heavy, the time and place we stood in history. We decided to climb to the top of the Tower of Silence and we stood outside those tall walls in front of a small opening. We didn't know if we were allowed to enter, but one by one, we stooped and snuck through anyway. There was nothing in there but stones and a blind sky overhead and the golden rays of a rising sun. Sarab started to sing in his clear, beautiful voice, "Mama, take this badge from me, I can't use it anymore. It's getting dark, too dark to see, feels like I'm knocking on heaven's door." And the rest of us sang, too, that Dylan song as eulogy for all the dead, the ones who had been laid to rest on those ancient stones, the ones who had fallen from the towers in New York, for all the dead that would soon be, once this war commenced. Then we walked a distance down the mountain toward the town, where Amir left to hire a small bus to drive us through the desert in search of Chak Chak.

While we waited, I watched a fruit seller set up for business, unloading a truck piled high with watermelon. A group of young laborers stood in the morning light, in a line, and a man in the truck threw a watermelon to the closest man to him, who threw it to the next, down the line, to the final man who piled it on wooden tables for sale. They spoke and repeated, "Ya Allah, Ya Allah," and laughed, their breath visible, sweating in the chill of the morning air. They were so alive in their bodies. So full of life. I walked up to the table and pretended to appraise the melons. A young, handsome laborer came to the table and, with skill, rapped his knuckle against a melon, another, and picked one up and handed it to me. "This one, abji," he said. "This one will be sweet enough for you."

I walked back to my friends waiting in the shade, holding my heavy, ripe melon in front of me like a pregnant belly, just as Amir finally returned. We drove out into the desert. For miles and miles, in complete emptiness. Not a tree, not a building, not a blade of grass, a walking soul, a single stray dog, no other cars. Nothing. Just a one-lane highway that stretched through purgatory. Then, the mountain came into view.

"The rest, you have to walk," the bus driver said.

At first, the footpath was rocky. I had my thirty-pound backpack on my back and my ten-pound melon in my arms, and the desert sun beating down on my head, the heat amplified beneath the fabric of my veil and hijab, with an uphill climb.

We arrived at stairs that rose through the jagged rocks, stairs made out of the mountain itself, carved into the stone. Endless stairs. I was panting, sweating, with that fruit clutched against my belly. It was an offering, I told myself, to the sahib of the temple, a gift so we wouldn't arrive as guests, empty-handed. The first terrace appeared, and roofed pavilions that served as accommodations for pilgrims. That first terrace led to more stairs that climbed higher and opened to other terraces and courtyards, which led to more stairs that opened to more terraces that led to more stairs. We climbed beneath the noon sun, until, finally, we came to the last set of stairs.

After those last few steps, we found ourselves standing before a pair of tremendous doors made of bronze, etched with the image of some ancient king, placed in front of a grotto in the heart of that mountain. Somebody in our group, maybe Sanam, audacious like that, thought to knock on the bronze door. It creaked open and, hesitantly, an old man peered out.

"What do you want?" he asked. He was dressed in all white. White skullcap on his sparse white hair. Loose white trousers, white kaftan over that. His eyes were pale, the dreamy eyes of the elderly. His gaze seemed elsewhere. He talked to us, but he talked beyond us, too. I walked forward and held the watermelon out to him. He took it from me, looked at me, and said nothing.

"We have come as pilgrims," Sanam said. "May we enter the temple?"

"Go away," he said. He turned and walked away slowly toward the stairs leading down, the watermelon in his hands.

"Please," Pouya said. "We've traveled a long way."

"You are not ready," he replied, without looking back.

"How can we become ready?" Amir called after him.

The old man returned, melonless and holding a heavy ring of keys instead. He chained and padlocked the doors to the temple as we pleaded and tried to persuade him to allow us entry. "You must first be purified," he said. He walked away again and we followed him this time, some of us telling him about our fatigue, others trying to prove our purity. Someone even offered him money, which he swatted away irritably. He walked down the steps, unperturbed by our voices, our insistence, then turned a corner, and we found ourselves standing in front of a long basin built into the wall of the mountain and lined with several golden faucets. Placed against the stone behind the basin was a long slab of mirror. I don't think I have ever seen a truer reflection of myself than the one in that old mirror, my face sweat-stained, dirty, with a desert, endless, stretching far behind me. The desert reflected in that mirror was wide, powerful, beautiful. And I, standing before it, small and powerful and beautiful and passing.

"Water," the old keeper said, nodding his head. Then, he walked away.

The miracles of those mountains are many. The story goes that an ancient princess, fleeing from hordes of invaders, came to this mountain, prayed to the great spirit of truth and wisdom, and a chasm opened and swallowed her before the awestruck army. In the bosom of that mountain ran a perpetual spring, which legend said was the flow of her eternal tears. Near the top of the mountain, within the grotto, there grew an old, old plane tree. Other trees grew there, too, outside of the temple, which shaded the pilgrims who came to worship. Within, a fire burned in an altar that had been tended by generations of keepers. We turned on the golden faucets to the miracle of water, clear and sweet, flowing from the tap. I washed my face, drank that water in my cupped hands, washed my arms, my neck, took off my dusty boots, my socks, hitched up my skirt and washed my tired feet. When everyone in our group was clean, we climbed back up to those closed bronze doors, to wait. After some time, the keeper came back out, walked past us without seeing us.

"We've been purified," Sanam said. "May we enter now?"

The old man stopped and squinted at us. "No," he said. "You are still not ready."

"What do we need to do now?"

"You are not humble enough." He unlocked the padlock, pulled away the chains, opened the door, entered the temple, then closed the door behind him. A few minutes later, he emerged, holding a basket full of small white skull caps. He handed them out to the boys, who put them on. We girls, humbled by Islam already, wore the veil of our hijab. Our heads covered, donning looks of humility, we waited outside the closed temple doors. Time passed. The old keeper waited beside us. Quietly. He looked off at the mountain. He looked at his fingernails. He pondered the gnats in a cloud of sanctimonious orgy. He hummed a little tune. And we resigned ourselves to waiting.

Finally, without explanation, the old keeper of the temple walked to the doors, took out the jangle of his keys, unlocked the padlock, pulled wide both sets of doors, then stood aside, his head bowed, as we silently filed in.

I would like to say that upon entering the temple, I was struck in the head by the lightning bolt of holy. It was beautiful, housed in that grotto. Inside hung a tremendous chandelier resplendent with crystals. Water dripped from the walls, *chak chak chak*. And, as promised, growing in the heart of that mountain was the thick trunk of an ancient tree, green, unlikely, miraculous, stretching out of an opening in the stone, toward the sunlight. I waited for the holiness to surge through me. But it didn't. We sat, the ten of us. Some in prayer, some in meditation. I walked up to the altar where the flame burned and tried to lose myself to the idea of an ever-burning fire. Nothing happened. Not even a spark. The old keeper watched me, closely, with those bygone eyes of his as I circled the altar and tried to force myself toward some sublimity. Finally, epiphany-less and bored, I left the temple, alone.

Since the place seemed empty, and the heat felt unbearable, I left my boots by the temple door, removed my hijab and veil, stuffed them in my backpack beside my boots, and walked away unencumbered and barefoot on those smooth, cool stones, my shoulders naked and my hair revealed, with the breeze on my skin.

I crossed through terraces, jumped across rooftops, climbed down a number of stairs until I turned a corner and suddenly found myself standing among a crowd of thirty or so young women, all dressed in full Islamic hijab, some with the more conservative chadors, gathered and talking quietly. A handful of those girls stood beside a giant cauldron and peeled in potatoes and carrots. An old man stirred the pot. Another girl fed the flame beneath it. Another sprinkled in salt. And there I stood among them, barefoot, bare shoulders and arms, hair flowing in the breeze. They all stopped what they were doing and stared at me. I tried to calculate the speed I needed in order to run and jump from that rooftop courtyard to another terrace, find the stairs leading back to the temple and plead for sanctuary, when the old man stirring the cauldron said, "Ah, our honored guest, you have arrived just in time for the feast."

The girls circled around me, dressed in their modest Islamic hijab, looked me up and down. Concluding accurately that I wasn't a local, they asked me where I was from, who I was, why I had come here, of all places.

"Say it again," they begged me.

"Los Angeles."

"Los Angeles," they repeated, imitating me by anglicizing the words with an almost Texan drawl. In Iran, they pronounce *Los Angeles* in its true Latin form, the way someone from Mexico might say it. When I named that place, said it the way we say it in LA, it seemed to these girls even more fantastic and foreign. They laid down a linen tablecloth on the stone floor and produced porcelain bowls and silver spoons.

"Our honored guest from America, you must sit at the head of our sofreh," the old man instructed me. These girls were volunteers for an organization much like the Red Cross. They fed the hungry, clothed the poor, helped those in need. The old man was their driver and chaperone, and they had come to this temple on a day trip. They invited me to sit at the head of their makeshift feast, and one of the girls brought me a bowl of lentil stew. Another one of the more conservatively dressed girls sat down beside me. She reached under the folds of her black chador, into her breast pocket and took out a little porcelain strawberry. She unscrewed the top, winked at me and sprinkled a red powder first in her bowl, then mine. "The old man makes the stews too bland," she whispered, as she quickly tucked the porcelain strawberry back into its secret place beside her heart, "and I like a little spice."

The girls asked me about this other world, this America, which they had only seen in movies, and heard about in stories and read about in the news. "Tell us," they demanded, "tell us how you live there."

I told them about the loneliness of my childhood as a refugee. I told them about my father, who worked hard to make us a home in that new place until he became ill, then withered and died, still a young man. I told them about studying at the university, and then the debts, the work, the futility. Then, I told them that I wrote poetry.

"Oh!" they cried, and they rushed to their backpacks and returned with journals and notebooks. "Write something, write something dedicated to me!"

So I did. Thirty personalized verses, at breakneck speed, while each girl whose notebook I held told me her story as I wrote her a poem.

"My father wants me to marry a man I barely know," one said.

"My parents won't allow me to attend university," another said.

"My older sister attempted suicide. She is married to a man who beats her, and no one will allow her to leave."

"I don't know what the future holds for me."

I sat among them, flooded by their stories, humbled, writing frantically, listening. I wanted so badly to give them something in return. For their hospitality, yes, but for more than that. For their beauty, for their trusting and open hearts. I wanted to give them something, some piece of me. I have a picture, a single photograph, the film long lost now. Sarab came upon us, followed by Pouya. The two of them found me sitting among the girls, scantily clad, in the shade of a tree, writing and writing. Before they wandered off, Sarab took out his 35mm camera, and took a picture. In that black and white photograph, I sit among those girls with my shoulders and arms revealed, and my hair showing. I'm looking down at a notebook. They sit around me, angelic, in all their innocent and beautiful glory.

After I wrote the last verse in the last notebook, their chaperone approached me, holding out three pomegranates. "The pomegranate that grows in the arid climate of Yazd is very different from any other in the world," he said. "It is said to be a barakat, a blessing. Take these as a gift from us." Then the girls embraced me, one by one, and kissed my cheek. And then they were gone, all thirty of them, the cauldron, the old man, the porcelain bowls, their voices. They had struck me, struck my heart with the lightning bolt of holy, and disappeared just as suddenly.

I sat for a while in the silence of their absence, full of the weight of all their stories, before I got up and hopped from one terrace across to the rooftop of another to search for the rest of my party. The sun was already sinking, so that the mountain glowed.

And that's when I saw him, sitting there, illuminated.

What I saw isn't anywhere in these words that follow, because a written account of an ineffable experience is an act of folly, though being human, and hence damned to both language and fallibility, I know no other way of explaining what happened and who he was. To understand, I'm asking you to suspend your knowing of things. Let go of all things you thought to be true, like the human form, the structure of time, the dictations of space, the idea of boundaries between life and death, and all the other concrete, tangible illusions that parade before us in this moment of transitory being. If you hold onto all that tightly, clutched in your hands, and say,

"This, *this* is reality," then this story will seem like the accounts of a young woman driven mad by grief. But what follows happened, and all those things, the body, time, death, space, it all unraveled when that man started to speak.

He must have been in his late forties. Forty-six, maybe, the same age my father died. He wore a shirt of heavy cloth, the color dulled by either the sun or too many washings. He sat in lotus position, facing the mountain, on the ledge of the rooftop, his back to the empty, blazing desert. He had dark hair, streaks of white in it, a rag tied around his temples. He could have been a beggar, or a junkie, or a thief hiding out in this lost place, he could have been broken or holy, but in that moment, he was clear, empty, in a place of peace, so I saw neither beggar, nor sage, nor thief. What I saw was a light emanating from him and I don't know, to this day, if it was something within him, or a trick of the desert, or a projection of my own longings, but that light drew me to him powerfully.

I watched him, at first, from a distance. Then, as though animated by something beyond myself, I jumped across the rooftops that separated us, walked up to him, and placed the three pomegranates at his feet. "The blessings of the arid earth," I said. "Some angels gave these to me."

Then, he spoke.

At one point, I knew all the ten members of our party sat there, listening. Night fell. A near full moon. A galaxy appeared overhead. "A time is coming," he said, and I saw fire, destruction, wasted earth, blood. "A time is coming," he said, and I saw chaos, suffering, children drowning in open seas, the hunger, and the thirst. "A nightmare awaits us, and we sit here on its eve, before the world begins the worship of fire." Then he looked at the sky above us, as though addressing it, and said, "But even between the tiger and the gazelle, there is Love."

I saw a tiger, like a flame, moving with stealth amidst the tall, golden grass of a savannah. He watched, enamored, the gazelle he hunted. The tiger thought of nothing but her grace. It heard nothing but the sound of her footfalls in the tall grass. The very air was the scent of her body. Then, the brilliant flash of her fear. And the chase. The struggle. The savage teeth against the taut skin, the torn flesh, the hot flow of blood, the intimacy of breath.

"Within this violence," the man said, "there is a hidden Love."

Someone made a fire. Beside its heat, we ate. When the desert became too cold to bear, the sage invited us into his room behind a tattered curtain that served as the fourth wall. A worn wool kilim on the stone floor, pillows, books, a blackened kettle. He made tea and offered us wisdom and cookies from a tin.

"It is not a time for drunkenness," he told us when someone pulled out a bottle of wine. "You must have your wits about you, for the illusions will be many. You will need a strong body and a strong mind to weather the storms." And then, at one point in the middle of those dialogues, he turned to me and, for the first time that evening, addressed me directly. "I am someone for you," he said. "Someone you seek through me. Tonight, you will make a gesture that will let me know who I am meant to be."

After the nearly full moon rose, the laughter of jackals echoed through the mountains. The moon gave way to the dark, impenetrable hours of the early morning, but the fire blazed with a gentle warmth, a gentle light. In those hours dedicated to sleep and dream, in lucid wakefulness, I leaned over to that stranger and I placed my hand on his shirt, my palm over his heart, then I looked him in the eyes. He let out a gasp, as though I had struck him, or as though he had just been witness to something awesome. He closed his eyes, nodded, sat still, and when he opened his eyes and looked back at me . . . an inexplicable familiarity. A remembering. He smiled. And I placed my head against his chest and wept. A fantastic light shone all around him, and he laughed.

I asked him, through my tears, "What am I going to do now?"

And he said, "You are going to live your life."

I can't explain. I don't know how. Madness, maybe. Later I would read the DSM, I'd read liturgies, study books on consciousness and on quantum theory, I'd talk to psychoanalysts, scientists, listen to lectures about hallucinations of the mind and reality, talk to the clergy of this and that religion. Years after, I would try to understand, to explain. But in the light of that dawn, he sat there before me. Forty-six, alive and in good health, though a bit thin. He was a man now, who lived in the mountains of a lost desert, at a temple with tremendous bronze doors, within which grew a miraculous tree and burned a miraculous fire and dripped from the walls the tears of an ancient princess. He sat before me, in the light of day, and I remembered him. Remembered the cadence of his speech. Remembered the glasses he pulled from his shirt pocket. Remembered the way he skinned an apple with a knife in one long, curling peel when I used to sit as a child and listen to his stories.

"How do I live my life, now that you are gone?" I asked him.

"With joy," he said, and laughed a laughter I remembered from before I even had memory. "A joy that comes from within you, from deep within you like a gushing spring."

He gave me a slice of the apple, and another, and another. He took the seeds from me and placed them in his shirt pocket, beside his heart.

"I've felt that joy," I told him. "Sometimes, it devastates me and all I can do is cry. Sometimes, it makes me want to dance, even in the streets."

"Then dance in the streets," he said.

"People will call me a fool."

"There are many ways of dancing," he said. "Remember the Charlie Chaplin movies?"

And I remembered sitting beside him on the couch as a child, my head in the crook of his arm, laughing with him at those silent black-and-white movies. "That was a dance, too," he said. "The art he created, it was a way of dancing, no?"

We walked up and down the stairs. We came to the temple doors. A crowd of pilgrims and Scandinavian tourists sat waiting, watching the old keeper impatiently. When the old keeper saw the two of us approach, he hurried past those people and, without a word, opened the bronze temple doors to let us in, then closed the doors, just as quickly, behind us as the crowd rose in protest, demanding to know why he let us in, and not them, even though they had been waiting all morning. We walked around and around the altar, talking. We danced, in conversation, so that we became nothing more than ideas, and past that, to something like light. Between us, a galaxy appeared. The sun climbed to its zenith. We opened the temple door to leave and the group of pilgrims and blond tourists sat resigned to waiting outside in the blinding light, beneath the shade of the trees. Amir sat among them, waiting for me.

"Is this paradise, then?" I asked the old keeper of the flame. He looked at me with his bygone eyes, and I saw the answer in them, before he turned to close the temple doors. I faced the pilgrims and the blond tourists, men and women with cameras around their necks and backpacks upon their backs, and questions in their eyes and sorrows in their hearts and I asked them, "Is it paradise you have all come seeking?"

The Scandinavian tourists looked at me uncertainly, but a group of pilgrims immediately surrounded me, asking, "What did you see within the temple, miss? What vision did you have? Did you hear a voice? What message do you bring?"

"That even a blighted desert can grow trees," I said.

He and I . . . that man . . . the Stranger, the thief, the sage . . . the one who allowed himself to become empty so that I could fill him with the spirit of the man I had been seeking and seeking . . . he and I . . . my father and I . . . we walked down those too few stairs carved out of the mountain, walked down the rocky footpath, walked until I saw the white tour bus waiting.

"I don't want to leave here," I said to him. "I want to stay with you."

"You must leave," he said. "There is a world waiting."

"And how do I face it, without you?"

"Look for me. You will find me." He reached into his pocket and took out the tiny, black apple seeds. He placed them in my hand. "Throw these in the dust," he said. "And from them springs a gallery of trees. There are so many paradises on this earth, waiting for you to see."

He walked me to the bus. He held my hand to help me in while Amir took my backpack.

"Allow that joy to rise within you," the man said. "Let it flow from you like a perpetual spring."

When the bus door closed, he raised his hand in farewell. My friends looked back at me . . . and they understood. Don't ask me how. Sometimes, it was like that, in that beautiful, tired, broken country of Iran. Sometimes, beyond all the chaos and the suffering, there was an element of the sublime so clear, it appeared before you as real as a mountain temple in a lost and endless desert.

WHILE OUR WHITE tour bus drove us through the desert back to the city and Amir read out loud from a little guidebook about a hotel named Malek-o Tojjar in Yazd's bazaar, I sat beside the window, watching the stretch of bleached landscape. My heart pounded in protest, the rhythm uncertain. I felt as though I couldn't inhale enough air, my thoughts hazy, my head swimming. "That hotel has been in business for over 250 years," Amir noted. "Longer than the United States has been in business."

Amir had sat waiting outside the bronze temple doors with the visiting pilgrims when I stepped out and the crowd surrounded me, asking what vision I had seen. It was then that he decided he needed to follow me more closely. And so when our party decided to split up and explore the city during the wait for our train, he offered to walk with me. Since I was having difficulty grounding myself, I figured it wouldn't hurt to let him carry my backpack and accompany me through the winding labyrinths of the bazaar.

The vendors in that bazaar, they all sang. They sang about their blackberries. They sang about the freshness of their poultry. They sang about the sale on tomatoes. They sang about hot chai. T-shirts, jeans, pots, radios, eggs. They sang about the variety of their melons. And amidst all this, there happened to be songbirds, too, hanging in little cages by the storefronts. Above all the human voices, I could hear the clear notes of the birds singing. I closed my eyes, leaned back against a wall, and listened to all of it, the haggling, the merchants, the birds, the scales, the coins, the people coming and going. There were the smells, too, of overripe cantaloupe, of ground cinnamon, the wafting smoke of wild rue seeds. And the dizzying sights. Whole skinned side of cow or an entire goat hanging from hooks, eyes bugged out and entrails dangling and delighted flies. The gleam of light in the gold merchants' windows. Entire stores dedicated to spools of thread. The bazaar offered commerce in its purest form. People smiled at one another. Sometimes, they yelled at one another.

They bargained, they talked politics, they gossiped, they argued. They were rude, gracious, kind. They praised the cut of meat. They boasted about the quality of their cotton. Something was alive in that place, full of life, there, something that didn't exist in the strip malls or supermarkets back in LA. There was a humanness to the exchange of cash for commodity. An intimacy between buyer and the seller.

On that afternoon's stroll through Yazd's bazaar, Amir and I came to a store that sold rock sugar. The window displayed what looked like giant, translucent gold gemstones. The confectioner stood by the door and looked at me like the grandfather I never had. He smiled in the warm glow of the light and invited me in to sample his sugar. Inside, he brought me a glass of tea, then chipped a piece of rock sugar with a small hammer and dropped it in my cup.

"Listen closely for the crackle," he said. "But do not stir. It is important to know the bitterness, first, in order to better understand the sweetness that follows."

I sipped my bitter tea. He asked me where I was from. "America," I responded.

"Is your family safe there?" he asked.

"My mother is frightened," I answered. "People are getting envelopes in the mail with anthrax. My uncles have put American flags on the windows of their cars, to indicate their loyalty, but people still yell and spit at them at stoplights, in the streets."

"It is a terrible, terrible tragedy. And now, America has decided to blame the Afghans. The Afghans! And soon, George W. Bush will begin the bombings," he said. His eyes teared, and he looked away. "How do you heal wrongdoing by doing wrong?" He shook his head. "We watched," he said. "We watched it, here in the market, those people falling from the towers in New York. Human life has no value for men in power, Taliban or American," he said. "They only think about money and mask their greed with righteous ideologies."

He stood up and filled a white box with rock sugar, then tied it with red string. "Take this to your mother as a gift from me," he said. "Tell her there is an old man in Yazd who believes that the bitterness will end, someday." By the time he handed me the box and bid me farewell, we already loved each other, that old man and I.

Amir and I walked down a particularly dark, long passageway that came to an end at a set of large wooden doors. Above the doorway, a sign read "Malek-o Tojjar Hotel. 250 years old." Amir pushed the doors and they opened to an expansive courtyard beneath the starry night sky. The two-story hotel was built around that open courtyard. In the middle was a long and shallow rectangular pool that reflected the night sky. The rooms above the courtyard had intricate latticed wooden shutters open to the night, and men and women sat on the balconies, drinking tea, smoking hookahs, talking in whispers. In a pavilion at the far end of the courtyard, beneath a canopy of jasmine, a group of men were gathered, sitting at tables, drinking tea. They, too, were talking, though passionately and out loud, in heated debate. There were no women there, it was clear that the pavilion and the dialogue beneath it was for men only.

I walked up closer to where I could unobtrusively listen to what they were saying. A young man spoke. "This is not a problem that can be resolved by war," he said. A chorus of voices agreed. "How do you heal atrocity by committing more atrocities, haji?" A louder agreement followed.

"No," a deep voice interrupted the crowd. He sat at another table, across from the young man's. He was older, tall, and heavyset. Judging by the size of the gold ring on his finger and the tailoring of his suit, it was clear that he was wealthy, this haji, who either owned a profitable business in the bazaar or was the very owner of the hotel itself. "No," the old haji said again, this time pounding the table with his fist for emphasis. "We cannot show weakness. If America decides to attack Iran as well, then we must fight to defend our nation."

"They will annihilate us," the young man said.

"Perhaps, but we will die with our dignity and our honor."

"Haji, what is dignity and honor to the dead?"

"It is everything." He had a look of impenetrable anger in his eyes. I watched the haji and the crowd of men awaiting the young man's response. Then, I noticed a small boy, a child, standing among the men, looking from one man to another. That little boy stood there, listening, learning, trying to piece together explanations of the world from what he heard these men say. He saw me, and I smiled at him. Here he was, so innocent. And what was he learning? Who would he hear? Which message?

"Haji?" I said, from the edge of that crowd. The men already knew of my presence. They pretended not to notice me out of respect, to protect my anonymity, but they knew I had been standing there for some time, they knew that I had been listening. But nobody was expecting that I would speak.

And I had the rules down by rote now. A woman should not be heard in public, not even the sound of her shoes. But didn't this moment, the moral magnitude of it, require that I speak? The men all turned to look at me. Amir looked ready to faint. I felt my heart in my mouth, and thought, *Well, if my heart is in my mouth, then it's through my heart that I should speak.* "Haji," I asked, "To what end? Where would your war lead us?"

He studied me for a moment, then asked, "Where are you from, young lady?"

"I am Iranian . . . but I grew up in America," I said. "So what does that make me, father? Your daughter or your enemy?"

That question was followed by a period of shocked silence. Not only because I dared to speak, but that I challenged a man older than me and placed him in a position that granted him one of two options, to either be hospitable and negate his own point, or to be rude to a guest, a young woman, publicly. The haji glared at me. Then, all at once, the other men started to speak before he had a chance to answer. A few men surrounded him and talked to him. A crowd of men surrounded me and apologized for the haji's opinions. Someone brought out another tray of tea and quickly passed it among the guests. The haji sipped his tea and looked at me while nodding his head in response to something someone said to him.

I reached into my backpack and pulled out the box of rock sugar. I opened it, walked over to him, and held out the box. "A bit of sweetness, to end the bitter," I said. And something in his gaze softened. Everyone watched, breaths shallow, waiting. Then, the haji reached over, took a piece, and dropped it in his tea.

It was time to catch our train. We bid everyone farewell, I bowed my head goodbye to the haji, who returned my gesture with a bow of his. On the way to the train, we passed through the produce section of the bazaar. I remembered the watermelon I had bought at the onset of this journey and thought it wise to buy more, so I purchased two. Then, we reluctantly boarded that Tehran-bound train out of Yazd, the fortnight before the commencement of a war that promised justice through the spilled blood of the enemy.

SOMETHING WAS WRONG with me. I think it may have been the full moon. Big and full and red, just shamelessly hanging in the black sky, ominous over that bleak desert as our train clackity clacked beneath it. I had never seen a moon like that. Red. Blood red. Like a pomegranate. It hung there, ironic and menacing. I walked past the open train compartment doors and asked the weary passengers if they had seen the moon that night. I felt a sort of existential recklessness. My heart wouldn't stop racing, perhaps because of the combination of heat exhaustion and fatigue from staying up the night before, but I could feel it pounding in my chest. I ambled through the halls of that train like a drunkard, peeking my head into compartments full of strangers, and asking, "Have you reckoned the moon tonight?"

Some passengers looked out of their windows and responded with awe. Some looked at me with awe, for behaving in a way a young woman on board a train in the Islamic Republic of Iran ought not to behave. Some passengers responded with verses of poetry learned by rote. Others, with biting sarcasm. But we all knew. All of us on board that train. We all knew that the war was about to begin. And nobody wanted that war. We had seen the Afghan refugees, broken, walking over the mountains into the cities of Iran to find work, to find safety from the slaughter of the Taliban. And there it hung in the black of night, that blood red omen of a moon. And somewhere, quite near, the American planes approaching and soon, very soon, the forecast of fire, raining from the skies.

I returned to my train compartment and found the watermelons I had purchased in the bazaar. I said to Amir, who hadn't left my side, "Let's invite everyone to the dining cart to share these melons."

By now, Amir seemed resigned to my dismissal of good sense, so without question he picked up the melons to follow me through the tight hallway as I invited strangers to meet us in the dining car, saying out loud, like some fruit merchant, "Come, come share the barakat, the blessing of melon." And what do you know, people came. We found ourselves in the dining car, a whole crowd of us, and I asked the waiter to bring me a sharp knife to slice those melons.

The gathering of a crowd of people is foremost among the many activities illegal in the Islamic Republic of Iran. Any gathering, unless it is sanctioned, like at a mosque or a funeral, is seen as a threat to the regime. Why? The Republic will have you believe that gatherings, particularly co-ed gatherings, are the hotbed of the devil and might lead good folks to sin. So they outlawed them.

The real reason is that when people gather, they talk. They discuss, they inspire, they mobilize. And on that particular night, driven by an existential drunkenness inspired by that blood red moon, I decided to hand out pieces of dripping watermelon on the rind as I delivered an inspired sermon about love. "It is time for an evolution," I told that crowd in the dining car. "It is time to forgo war and bloodshed, to rise above barbarism and become fully human, compassionate, forgiving . . ." They agreed out loud, listened with rapt attention, and I felt I had found my calling. I was meant to be a revolutionary. And I would bring about change, I would shift the culture of violence and bloodshed to one of friendship and amiability through watermelon. It was that easy.

And it was, really. Just like that. I cut some melon, invited strangers to sit around and talk, and there we were, friends raised from our collective depression and helplessness to a place of solidarity. There's something to be said about that naïveté, that wholehearted foolishness. That faith, that grandiosity, that belief in the world and in yourself, that hope that comes with youth. It's a beautiful place. And from it comes something powerful. But you know, and I know now, that my watermelon did not bring the new world order as I envisioned that night on board that train, heading toward the commencement of a brutal and senseless war and everything that followed. But it planted some seeds. Who's to say that someday we won't stand in that paradise?

I'll tell you who. The guard who marched into the dining car, in his green soldier's uniform, with his rifle on his shoulder. Erect. Formal. "You must disperse immediately," he said.

And I said, "Come, brother, come and share the barakat of friendship and love with us."

And he said, "Everyone, return to your compartments immediately."

And I said, "But we are talking about love, and the evolution of humanity toward the light of unity."

And he said, "Now."

And just like that, the people gathered grew smaller with fear, shrunk into themselves, into shadows of themselves, and hung their heads, and began walking away. "But, brother," I began. And then I saw. That boy in that uniform had nothing in his eyes. They were empty, his focus beyond us, his soul replaced by the orders that had been drilled into him. He couldn't see friends, or love, or dripping, sweet watermelon on the rind. He saw a crowd of rogue dissidents. A danger to the regime. A threat. And that rifle was now clutched in both his hands. And things change when a rifle speaks. A few kind strangers felt the need to hush me up and guide me back to my compartment as quickly as possible.

"You can't explain anything to those boys, miss," they told me.

And maybe it was that full moon, or the eyes of that young child in the old hotel who listened to the haji demand the blood of the enemy, but I wasn't done talking. So I did. Out loud, through the tight hallways of that train, past the open compartments with gawking strangers, followed by my crowd of curious congregants, back to my compartment, where I continued, "That soldier was once a wide-eyed boy who listened to the wrong story. And that is why, for humanity to evolve collectively, we must first teach the children about love, and allow them to grow toward this light."

I carried on like that for the duration of the train ride. I sat in my compartment, full of strangers listening beside me, strangers standing in the doorway, crowded down the hallway. I carried on and on about love, about compassion and forgiveness while that train carried us back to the city and the world carried us right into that war. And I'm still waiting. Even though I'm not her anymore, that drunken, foolish child with her watermelon and her grandiosity, and her dream, I'm still waiting. And who's to say? Who's to say that someday, the paradise she sought won't come into being?

AS THE UNITED States began the siege of Afghanistan, Behrooz said he felt a tiredness he had never felt before. Amir professed his devotion to me, while Ramin the photographer wouldn't answer my attempts to reach him. My mother called in the mornings. "Things are strange here," she said. "America is changing." Javid suggested we go trekking to the village of Shahsavar. Behrooz asked Javid, for the first time, to lead the trip. We left the city without Behrooz.

On the first night, we camped beside a river, beneath a lightning storm that illuminated the skies. The next night, we swam in a cave that hid a pool fed by hot springs. To reach the village of Shahsavar the following morning, we had to walk through the cemetery first. Moss-covered tombstones nearly hidden in the tall, dew-drenched grass, some so ancient, the elements had returned them to their original form of stone. Below that mountain cemetery, through the fog, there was a glimpse of a lush, green valley full of rice paddies.

In the stillness of that morning, in the golden rays of the rising sun that pierced the dissipating mist, we heard the sound of a young girl's voice singing. Her song came from one of the rice paddies below and echoed through those mountains. Clear. Sweet. Holy. We stopped, our whole group, in reverence, and listened as she sang. Somewhere, in the world beyond that village, there was war. But on that morning, just her song, which rose with clarity above the blanket of fog, transcended the gravity of death and forgotten tombstones, dismissed the very mountains and reached heaven.

After we returned to Tehran, Behrooz held up his right arm and said he felt a loss of strength in it. Sarab invited professional musicians to play with us in the afternoons. Bass guitarists. Percussionists. A boy magnificent on the trumpet. He asked them what they thought of our sound. We talked about recording and found a recording studio downtown. In the soundproof room among the microphones and the instruments, the sound engineers watched from behind the glass as the musicians improvised and I wailed my poetry.

The next night, Amir showed up at my door unexpectedly. He held a daf in his hand, the giant orb of that percussion encircled by a thousand brass rings. Without coming in, he told me he had driven several hours to some far-flung town to the ceremony of an order of Dervish to meet with their elder to buy this particular daf, which was more than a hundred years old and known to be very powerful. He told me he had persuaded the old man to sell it to him. He stood outside the door, offering me that instrument in his outstretched hands, the wood of the frame almost golden, the surface of the goat skin dappled like the full moon. I took it from him and the thousand small brass rings around the frame sounded with a resonance so deep, I felt it in my bones. "This instrument has waited a century to find you," Amir told me.

No one knew Ramin's whereabouts.

Behrooz and his wife visited doctors.

Each night, when I put my head on the pillow, I could hear my own heartbeat, the rush of blood in my ear. The rhythm irregular. I thought about the holes before falling asleep. Each morning, my mother called. "It's strange," she told me. "The American flag everywhere you look."

On the American newscasts, the reporters spoke of freedom and missiles, bombings and democracy. Patriotic music played to the footage of the green streak of an airstrike across the black of night, and the sudden light that appeared when that missile landed among the sleeping inhabitants of some Afghan city.

The doctors ran several tests on Behrooz.

At night, my heart a racket of sound, no discernable pattern, a frenzied din.

Ramin the photographer kept silent.

Amir wouldn't stop calling.

The street sweepers swept the orange and gold sycamore leaves, and those leaves kept falling. In the late afternoons, I walked in the streets. One evening, after the azaan, I came upon a funeral procession outside a mosque. Men and women in black, weeping, chanting along with the roseh khan, pounding their chests in unison. I stood outside of their crowd, dressed in orange and gold, watching. A woman in a black chador, tears on her cheek, turned around and spat at me feet. "Kaffir," she called me.

I called Ramin the photographer, again. "I'm coming over," I said into his answering machine. I called a cab. I arrived in his neighborhood. I couldn't remember which apartment, among those crowded apartments, was his. "I'm here, somewhere on your street," I said into his answering machine. An old dervish sat on the sidewalk beside the payphone. He held out his copper begging bowl to me. I filled it with coins and said, "I've come seeking a friend I cannot find. Will you pray for me?"

"That same Friend is seeking you, daughter," he said, and just then, Ramin turned the corner, and stood before me.

"You haven't killed yourself, then?" I said.

"No."

"Well, you had me worried."

"Let's get out of here, somewhere quiet, to talk."

Outside of Tehran at a nearby village, we carried a blanket, a handheld cassette player, a few tapes, a kettle, and some bread and cheese into an orchard of apple trees, the ground carpeted with brown, orange, gold brittle leaves. A young man there offered to walk us to a nice spot at the top of the mountain where he spread the blanket beneath an apple tree, gathered kindling, made a fire, filled our kettle from a spring, looked at me, smiled and said, "Isn't it miraculous?" he said. "This gallery of trees, sprung from seeds someone threw to the earth?" Then, he turned and left. And there, beneath that apple tree, Ramin the photographer asked to marry me.

I didn't answer. I pretended he was joking. I changed the subject. I told him about my heart instead. That I needed surgery. "I haven't told anyone else yet," I said. "Nobody knows there's something wrong with me." Ramin smoked his pipe. We listened to music on the cassette player. We drank tea, then lay on the blanket beside one another and looked at the sky through the tapestry of leaves.

The young village man returned on the back of a white mule just before sunset. "I thought you might need help walking back down," he addressed me. He picked an apple from a tree, rinsed it with the water of the kettle and handed it to me. Then he gathered an armload of apples and filled my backpack with them. The village man and I argued about the merits of his white mule versus a BMW as he led us down the curving, tight trail alongside the mountain. The sun set and the stars appeared and Ramin walked behind us, smoking quietly.

At night, the urgency of my heart kept me from sleeping. In the mornings, my mother said, "We are not welcome anywhere we go, not in the markets, not in the restaurants, not on the streets." Behrooz's test results revealed nothing. Ramin the photographer called, but didn't mention that afternoon beneath the apple trees. Amir called. "Come out with me tonight. Let's go downtown, get some coffee. I want to talk to you about something."

The Iranian newscaster on the coffee shop television numbered the civilian deaths in Afghanistan as Amir sat gazing at me. I felt like I was suffocating. "I'll be right back," I said. I fled into the street. It was dark. The headlights of cars. The shadows of strangers. The air thick with exhaust. There was nowhere to go, and I couldn't breathe. I walked back in and just as I passed the barkeeper who stood watching the TV and absently drying a glass with a rag, an old man on a barstool at the counter stopped me. He had blue eyes, white hair, wore a tweed jacket, a fedora. He reached out his hand, tapped my shoulder as I passed and said, in English heavy with an Eastern European accent, "You are a Sagittarius."

"How did you know?" I asked.

"I can see."

He talked, at length, about the constellations and universal frequencies, vibrations that spoke between heavenly bodies. Finally, he took my palm in his hand and studied it.

"Am I dying?" I asked him.

He didn't answer me for several minutes, just held my open palm, reading. "You will die on a Friday afternoon. On the nineteenth of October. At the age of ninety-three. You will be sitting among a group of young people, talking beside a fountain in an old courtyard. You will retire to your room to rest on your bed. You will look at the window, the curtains of which will blow in the breeze. You will hear the sound of the water splashing in the fountain, bird song, the laughter of those young people. You will close your eyes, then fall asleep."

"How do you know?"

"Go upstairs. That young man is waiting," the old man said. "Soon he will ask you a question, and you will say no."

"No to what?"

"To who he wants you to be."

I walked upstairs to the table where Amir was waiting. He gazed at me with a terrifying adoration, but before he opened his mouth to speak, I said, "Let's leave." When we walked back down the stairs, the old man was gone. The barkeeper dried another glass, his eyes fixed on the TV.

I could no longer sleep. My mother's calls in the mornings felt like a strange and repeating dream. "When will you come home?" she asked me. Behrooz grew weaker, more tired. The death tolls rose. Along the avenues were mountainous piles of orange and gold sycamore leaves and the street sweepers beside them, damned to their eternal and futile sweeping.

I BOOKED MY ticket back to Los Angeles.

"I have to go back home," I told everybody. "I need to have open-heart surgery. I'll return as soon as I can. This is where I want to be, once things have settled and I heal. Tehran is where I need to be."

Mehrabad Airport, Heathrow, LAX.

Outside of customs, my mother embraced me. We drove home in the deadlocked traffic of the LA dusk. The sun hung heavy in the sky, a large, orange, stagnant disc in the haze of exhaust and fumes. Its light reflected blindingly from the sea of metal surrounding us. Horns. Screeches. Newscasts, music, commercials. People sat behind steering wheels, their eyes fixed forward, weary, impatient. Broken. The cars all had flags affixed to them, taped to their windows, stuck on their bumpers. The billboards along the highway were plastered with flags, too. *G.d Bless America,* they read.

I told my mother about the prognosis, the holes in my heart. "Why didn't you tell me sooner?" she yelled at me, clutching the steering wheel.

"I didn't want to worry you."

"You could have died!"

"Look, I'm fine. It's nothing."

The next morning, she called my cardiologist. We met with him, he advised a more accurate procedure to identify the size and the location of the holes before we scheduled the surgery. A few days later, Justin called me.

"You're back," he said.

"For a minute, only," I said. "I need to have open-heart surgery."

"Don't you want to see me?"

That night, we sat in my parked car on a quiet suburban street. "I've recorded some of my poetry with a group of musicians," I told him. He didn't respond. He wouldn't look at me. "And I've sort of figured out what I want to do, you know, with my life. I want to work with kids. Help them, you know, make sense of the world. I still don't know how, but I know it has to be something like that, you know? Something to do with kids . . . and making the world a better place, and hope . . ."

"What about me?" he said.

"What do you mean?"

"Have you forgotten all about me?"

"No . . . No . . . I haven't forgotten you."

"It seems you've moved on. Without me."

"I . . ."

"Did you sleep with anybody?"

"What? I'm . . . I mean there's some guys . . . I dated . . ."

"Did you sleep with them? Did they touch you?"

"Well . . ."

"You're mine, still. You know that, right? You belong to me. I want to sit closer to you. I need to feel you next to me. Get in the backseat."

"I have to go back in, soon. My mother is waiting. I'm on Tehran time, still. And I have this procedure in the morning."

He got out of the car, opened my door.

"Just for a minute, you owe me that. A minute," he said. "I just want to feel you next to me." He held the door open, waiting. "Get in the back. Just for a minute. Please."

I got out. He didn't look at me. I sat in the backseat. He got in and closed the door. He kissed my neck. He kissed my face. His hands groped me. "Remember?" he said into my ear. "Remember, how you belong to me?"

"I have to go," I said.

He kept his eyes averted as he pushed himself on top of me.

"I need to go, please," I said.

My breath fogged the glass of the backseat window. The street outside. Suburban. Quiet. The houses dark. Their doors locked. Too late in the night for anybody to walk by. Nobody returning home. Nobody leaving. The moon was the only witness, pale and waning. The trees lining the street stood bare, their naked limbs spread wide across the dark skies. I watched the trespass of leaves across mowed lawns. Not a soul walked by that parked car. And even if they had, I don't think I would have screamed.

"There *is* something wrong with your heart," he said, pushing himself onto me. "You don't know how to love."

I didn't scream.

I said, instead, "I don't want to. Stop, please. Please?"

"You're mine," he said. "Right? Right?"

After a while, I stopped struggling, and then, I stopped pleading. He wouldn't look at me. He finished. He pulled away from me. When I breathed, my breath fogged up the glass and wiped out the neighborhood, the sidewalk, the homes, the trees. I focused on just that, my breath on the glass, and the world, disappearing.

THE NEXT MORNING, I awoke to the sound of my mother in the kitchen cooking with the television on in the background. From outside came the racket and din of lawnmowers and leaf blowers. From a nearby schoolyard came the voices of children playing. The newscaster announced that we were on orange alert for that day. I pulled back the curtain and looked out my bedroom window at the rows of quiet houses beneath a cloudless, blue sky. The night before, I had walked into my mother's house, walked straight to my room.

"You're back?" my mother asked from the living room.

"I'm tired," I said. "I'm going to sleep." Quietly, I closed my bedroom door and sat on the edge of the bed for a long time. Then, Amir called me. He had called, without fail, every night since my return.

"Did you meet with Justin tonight?" he asked me. I couldn't find my voice. I didn't want to speak. "Did something happen?" he asked. "You can tell me. Did something happen to you? Did he hurt you? I knew he would, when you told me he wanted to see you, I knew he would harm you. Did he yell at you, threaten you? Did he hurt you?"

". . ."

"You can tell me. You must tell me. Please?"

"He raped me."

". . ."

After breakfast that morning, we drove to the UCLA Medical Center. On the corner of Westwood Boulevard and Wilshire, there stood a high-rise building with a mural painted on its side of a female soldier, fatigues buttoned tight over her ample breasts, dark-skinned, lips plump and glistening. In the painted background, a desert, flames, helicopters, explosions, a soaring eagle, talons spread.

"You can wait for her out here," the nurse told my mother when she rose to follow me into a dim room full of medical equipment and computers and screens. A crowd of busy people jostled around, preparing. The nurse asked me to swallow something, then to lie on a table. A doctor stood beside her, clipboard in hand, with a group of students behind him, clipboards in hand, a technician waiting.

The doctor introduced himself to me as the head of the congenital heart disease center. The bright-eyed students waited. "We need to determine the exact positioning of the holes in your heart, and to measure their size," the doctor told me. The students scrawled frantic notes. "This test is more precise than the echocardiogram. We insert a tube through your mouth, it travels down your throat, and allows us a clearer view of your heart. That way, when you go in for surgery in a few weeks, the surgeon will know the precise nature of what we are dealing with." He didn't even look at me directly when he spoke. I was an exhibit. He delivered his presentation and the students took notes, eagerly. "It will only take a few minutes. You will be awake through the procedure, but we have given you sedatives to both relax you and keep you from moving your arms and legs."

The room became hazy. I felt a heaviness in my body. Suddenly, a number of hands were touching me. Men and women in blue scrubs surrounded me, masks over their faces, their eyes averted. They lifted my arms, my legs, turned me to my side, plunged needles into my veins, dripped liquids into me, taped wires to my skin, ignored me when I flinched, ignored me when I moaned.

"It will be uncomfortable," the doctor said from a far, far distance.

"Just for a minute."

He never looked at me. He never looked me in the eyes. The whole time. Not during. Or after. He kept his eyes from me.

"Okay, we're ready to begin."

I wouldn't have screamed.

But it wouldn't have mattered, even if I had.

They waited, took notes, watched the machines attached to my body, read numbers and lines on the screens. They touched my body with gloved hands. Then, the technician inserted something into my mouth. I didn't see the instrument, but immediately, I wanted him to stop. He didn't. He ignored me when I moaned, when I gagged, when tears streamed down my face in protest. He never looked in my eyes to see. He heard my protests. But he didn't listen. He kept pushing it in. I was drowning. Frantic. Animal. Paralyzed. I couldn't raise my hand to push him away. I couldn't raise my foot to kick. I could not make a fist. He kept his eyes from me and pushed it deeper, until he reached my heart and saw the holes.

The doctor said, "Here. Here it is. The malformity."

I couldn't scream. And then it was over.

I lay on that table, weeping.

SOME DAYS WERE yellow. Other days, orange. Some days, red. They announced which color the day was destined to be with great trepidation and foreboding on the radio and the TV. I stayed in my room. "I'm tired," I told my mother.

I sat on my bed and watched the shadows creep along the wall. It was so quick, the change in me. It was so sudden. All of it. Mehrabad, Heathrow, LAX. The parked car. The gloved hands. The intrusions upon my body. And now I sat bereft and broken, through the length of the day. Who was that girl, the outspoken one among the men in that old hotel, the revolutionary on board that train? The one who braved the desires of her body and swam in the open, blue sea? How had she felt so happy? So unafraid? So certain and so whole? And now . . . now I sat in my room on a Tuesday or a Monday afternoon. I didn't want to answer the phone. I didn't want to leave the house. The world outside was on alert for disaster, apprehension and fear and mistrust thick as the morning smog that hung over the city. Even my own body felt alien to me. What was this thing that had betrayed me? That had allowed such terror to be acted upon it, that had invited such intrusions, and now held me hostage to the fear of pain and death?

My mother returned at night to find me sitting in the dark. Every two weeks, she drove me back to the UCLA Medical Center, where I would sit in a chair while a needle plunged into my vein took blood from me and collected whole pints of it in a large plastic bag to save for my transfusion post-surgery. On the way home, I sat pale, exhausted, dizzy beside her as she drove. "It's no use trying to find a job right now," she told me. "With all the medical appointments, then the surgery. It can wait. Why don't you call up some of your old friends so you're not so lonely? Justin, maybe?"

I sat in my room, waiting.

Amir called every evening. Ramin the photographer called, too, every few days. Other than that, entire days passed without anyone speaking to me. One day, on our way home after the bloodletting, I noticed that the city of Beverly Hills was already decorated with tinsel for the holidays. We drove past Bloomingdale's. In the storefront window, there was a group of female mannequins arranged in what appeared to be a harem, within a domed tent of richly colored silk. Dark haired. Veiled faces. Fashionably wide pants paired with midriff tops. The mannequins reposed with their stiff limbs, splayed out on ottoman cushions and thick Persian rugs, waiting, as the radio announced the updates on the Taliban, Bin Laden, the bloodthirst of the Middle East.

On TV, the war looked like a show of lights. The reporter stood, mic in hand, and behind him streaks of neon-green light flashed across the dead skies. Then, a sudden light among distant buildings. No close-up of the rubble and the bones in the wake of that shooting star. No wailing mother over the broken body of her child. Just that silent light falling from heaven. Watching it, you would think it didn't even disturb the sleep or the dreams of the inhabitants of that darkened city.

The heart surgeon explained to my mother and me how all the functions of my body would be transferred to a machine during the eight to ten hours of my surgery. I couldn't stop crying. "But where will I *be* during those hours?" I asked the surgeon. "Once you take my body, where will *I* be?"

Behrooz, his wife, and Pouya visited us in Los Angeles. The authorities wouldn't allow Javid to leave Iran. When Behrooz pulled into our driveway and stepped out of the car, I threw myself into his arms. He held me for a long while in his embrace, kissed the top of my head. "Don't worry," he told me. "This is just another part of your journey."

Pouya had brought me a VHS tape from Ramin the photographer. That night, alone at home, I put it in the VCR and watched. The film began with the static of analog, the noise, the black-and-white snowstorm, before it cut to still photos of me. I sat in a café we used to go to. The lighting was soft. A photo of me looking out of the window. Another smiling at the camera. Looking pensive. Laughing. Holding my head. Readjusting my hijab. There was a montage of close-up photographs of my lips, several of the freckles on my face, of my hands, my fingers. Abruptly, the film cut from the still photos in that café to the footage of that day Ramin and I spent in a village among the apple trees, when he asked me to marry him. The camera focused on a herd of sheep walking down a distant path. A shepherd stood afar, watching over them. It was dusk, autumn, and the leaves spectacular. The camera turned to me. I was talking to a handsome, young village man who sat on top of a white mule. The camera zoomed in on my face, until it faded. The film cut to black.

I didn't know her. That girl in the tape. I searched and searched the emptiness inside me, and I couldn't find her. When Ramin called, I was embarrassed to talk to him, afraid he might hear the hollowness in my voice. On those phone calls, my laughter was forced. My bravado flimsy. I dreaded being asked what I was up to. I was up to nothing. I sat all day, waiting. And I didn't know what I was waiting for. Death, maybe. Something in me was gone. Something, taken from me. Justin called. Once or twice. After that night, I didn't answer. On New Year's Day, I left my room, got into the car, and drove to the coastal mountains he and I used to hike. I walked off the trail to a path through the sage, up the mountain, to a boulder overlooking the creek below. I stood on the edge of that boulder for some time, just stood there, looking down at the granite rocks within that gorge, the trickle of water passing in the creek.

Before Behrooz left Los Angeles, I told him I wanted to show him the northern redwood forests. We drove several hours north, then walked together into that forest, into the ferned gullies, among the thick roots, the tangled growths that pushed through rock and hill, among the salmon, sala-manders, slugs, pebbled brooks, cold rivers, rotting logs. It kept raining. "It is okay to be frightened," Behrooz told me in a cathedral of giant, ancient trees. "I'm frightened, too. The weakness has spread to my left arm. When I return to Tehran, they will run more tests, but I won't allow fear to stop me from living."

Behrooz, his wife, and Pouya returned to Tehran. Amir called, every night. His voice, a hypnotic soliloquy. "You are brave," he told me. "You are beautiful. Special. You will come back to Iran, soon, and be who you were meant to be."

Then, one day, Ramin sent me an email. It read, "Remember that afternoon when you told me the story of your golden fisherman? I went to Feraydoon Kenar. I found him for you. I told him you sent me, to say hello. His real name is Majid. I asked him if I could take a picture of him for you. Attached to this email."

I opened the attachment. And there he was. Standing beside his red boat, in front of that blue sea. I don't know if it was the angle of the lens. Or the lighting. But there was nothing golden about the man in that photograph. He was just a man. Tired looking. Ordinary.

"How dare you?" I yelled at Ramin on the phone. "What right did you have to intrude yourself into my story, and take it from me?"

I WENT IN for surgery on February 14, 2002. Valentine's Day. They let me pick the date. We arrived at the UCLA Medical Center at five in the morning, my mother and I. There was already a crowd of people waiting outside the door. We were all pre-op, or families of people who were pre-op, all of us standing quietly in the subdued gray of the morning.

Later, hooked up to my IV, I waited. The waiting went on for a long time. At noon, a nurse walked in and apologized. The surgeon had two emergency operations before me. A couple more hours, she told me, and it would be my turn. And I guess it was then, lying there in that room waiting, that I thought of all those days I had sat alone in my bedroom, waiting. Afraid. And now, they would finally take my body. Take me from my body and do things to it. And there was nothing I could do to stop them. There was no use in pleading, or in struggling. My mother stood in the doorway, crying, as they wheeled me out. We entered a room cluttered with things I couldn't make out. I asked if they had put me in a closet of sorts, for later. They laughed until the ceiling seemed to dissipate into nothing.

I OPENED MY eyes. The only light in the room was a glaring one, directly above my bed. The rest of it a dark, empty stage. Around my bed droned the machines, with lights that blinked on and off, and things that pumped, and alarms that rang every so often, which brought the man with the angelic face back into view. He hovered above me, around me, adjusted things, looked at me quietly.

Coming to felt like rising from the bottom of a blue sea and trying to surface too fast. My body screamed its ascent back into consciousness, *too much pain, better stay here, in the deep, deep void.* But I opened my eyes and saw his face. I was certain I had seen him before. Maybe in a car that had stopped on a long, deserted highway near the Canadian-US border, in the middle of some night of my childhood. My mother was a young woman walking toward that car, holding my hand. The car door opened and a man and woman asked my mother if she needed a ride. When we got in and started driving in the direction of America, a little boy with golden hair popped up from the front seat, from between his parents, and held out a stick of gum to me. Was this man that little boy? Older now, though angelic, still?

"Where is my mother?" I asked him.

"She is asleep, in a chair, here, beside your bed."

"Is she okay?"

"She is exhausted. I gave her a pillow and a blanket."

"Will you marry me?"

When I awoke again, he was at the foot of my bed. I could hear his voice, talking to another man. There were other beds in that darkness, other machines pumping, droning, screaming in alarm. "She needs a blood transfusion," the other man said.

Thirst.

The thirst woke me. The light glared above my bed, and my throat burned with thirst. Clenched upon itself, a pain so acute, it quieted all the other pain in my body and all I could think was *water.*

"Please. I'm so thirsty," I said to him when he appeared.

"The IV will keep you hydrated," he said.

"Just some water?"

"I can't give you any, not yet. You'll vomit immediately. You won't like that too much."

"Please? Just a little? Please?"

He was gone. I closed my eyes. The thirst. It is impossible to describe it with words. A desert blighted my mouth. A wretched storm of sand filled my throat. Broken glass. The constriction of the throat. My whole body ached for water, screamed for it. Then.

Then I stood on what seemed like the edge of somewhere, a cliff, and beyond it, a darkness. Not a sea of darkness, because a sea was a something. It was a nothingness and it had a pull to it. I thought, *if I should step off this ledge, here, and fall into these depths, then there will be no more thirst. There will be no more pain. Or fear.* And it seemed like the easiest thing in the world to do, to just leave behind my body. Nothing terrible or violent about it. Nothing foreboding or secretive or awesome, even. Just, nothing. Death was that easy. One breath less, and I could just not be. And since being meant so much suffering, since being was an unquenchable thirst, I thought, *how easy*, and I wasn't afraid.

He was standing beside my bed again. "Here," he said. "I brought you some water." He dipped a cotton swab in a glass of water and brought it to my lips. "I'll wet your mouth with it. It's all I can give you, for now."

I opened my mouth.

It was a drop.

A single drop of water. That's all. And the pleasure of that single drop . . . I felt it on my tongue, and the wave of it broke against every cell in my body and all I could think was *more*. Just that, a single drop of water, and the hope, the longing to feel that pleasure, again . . . It was the immensity of that desire which pulled me away from the edge of nothingness, of darkness, and brought me back to being.

AT NIGHT, THE other patients, mostly elderly women, drifted through the walls and into my room. They hovered by my bedside, talking endlessly about their pain, their grievances, their regrets. In the mornings I told the new nurse in attendance that I couldn't sleep. I begged to be taken off the morphine. "I see ghosts," I told the nurse. "All night they talk to me."

"I'll mention it to the doctor," each new nurse promised me.

The morning after my surgery, a group of doctors came to my bedside, followed by note-taking residents with clipboards in hand and stern smiles plastered on their faces. "We are going to remove this tube in your neck," one told me. They huddled around me, forgot me, spoke to one another. I was no longer in possession of my own body. It belonged to these strangers, these men and women with their white coats and their gloved hands and stern smiles. Somebody tugged and slid that tube slowly out of the flesh of my neck. The pain made me faint. They revived me and gave me more morphine. The next day, another group of doctors wanted to pull out the tubes that drained the liquid around my surgical site. The ones beneath my breast, under skin and flesh and bone. It was the kind of pain that swallowed screams, the shock of my body's capacity for suffering so intense, it left me catatonic, mute, wide-eyed with wonder. The next day, they came to pull out wires attached to my heart to measure something that didn't need measuring anymore. It became so that each time I heard footsteps stop outside my door, I'd start shaking uncontrollably, sweating, unable to breathe.

One night, tired of listening to the old women who congregated above my bed, I excused myself politely from their company and tried to get up. I managed to sit. Then, to stand. I took one step toward the light coming from the open door. Steady. My body screaming with pain, even through morphine. One step more. One more step, and another, and another, until I reached the threshold, held the door frame, and looked into the glaring light of the quiet hallway, where nobody floated around, talking. But then, the ground started to swell, like the waves of a sea, and the walls grew farther and farther and suddenly, black.

The next series of sensations were an onslaught. Sharp smell, water, hands, someone slapping my face, lights shined directly into my eyes. "Do you know your name?" they asked me. "Do you? What's your name?"

"Tell us your name. Do you remember your name?"

"Do you know where you are?"

"Do you know why you are here?"

"Do you remember? Do you remember who you are?"

I stood in a place bereft of time. They held my body, back in my bed now, and crowded around me with their frantic, unfamiliar faces, measured things and spoke to one another about numbers and shook me and jostled me and touched me and I stood far from it, in that place bereft of time. I heard their question, "Do you remember your name?" And I couldn't. For a moment, I couldn't remember who I was. And

I thought, *if I could just recall my name, from that, I might be able to find the rest of me.*

I DON'T REMEMBER much from those early days of my recovery, once I returned to my mother's home. Just the miracle of blue skies when I awoke each morning. I opened my eyes, pulled back the curtains and saw, once more, blue skies, and thought to myself, *How many miracles befall me each minute that passes, a miracle to be alive.*

But I was afraid. The world outside was beyond me. I couldn't even inhabit my own body. It hurt too much. And I was afraid of its treachery, its capacity for pain and suffering. I was afraid of my own heartbeat. I was afraid of that scar beneath my breast. Raw and swollen, with black seams and tape. I worried that if I moved too fast, or coughed too hard, or raised my arm, the seams would come undone, that it would split open to reveal flesh and rib. That dark things would come spilling out of me. It was too delicate, that body, too frail. I became afraid of movement. Of standing. Of walking. Of carrying things in my hand. I lay in bed, drugged, the whole day and watched the shadows creep along the wall.

I spent many nights in the hands of emergency room nurses and doctors those first couple months. They ran back and forth, watched screens, took blood, waited with machines ready to revive me if I flatlined. One night, after I was released, a nurse wheeled me out just as another gurney was being rushed in. A young man in it, unconscious. The people administering to him shouted, ran, yelled numbers and jargons. "Motorcycle accident," they announced to one another. Despite their urgency, the speed at which they moved, he passed me in the rift between moments, so slow that I saw the peace of his sleep, the beautiful structure of his chin and cheeks, the stubble of a beard, the closed eyes beneath thick lashes, the glitter of shattered glass embedded in his skin. He was so beautiful, that cursed prince in his deep slumber. Bloodstained and broken. Torn jeans and jagged limbs. Beautiful and grotesque in his fragility. He would die. And I would die. And that was the story of the human body.

My mother helped me into the car. I couldn't hold my head up, so I leaned my cheek against the cold passenger window and looked out into the night as we drove down Westwood Boulevard. At a red light, a maître d' stood in a tuxedo before a fancy restaurant, the valets rushing, the patrons waiting, dressed up in fine clothes, laughing and talking, dreaming themselves immortal in the golden light of the street lamps and the theater marquees. I looked at them and wanted to roll down my window and scream, "You don't know how close death stands! Closer than that man who touches your bare shoulder with his hand! Closer than the breath of that woman as she whispers her brazen words into your ear! Death is closer to you than all the longings you feel coursing through your own body!"

AMIR CALLED. EACH and every night. His voice, a hypnotic soliloquy. "You are brave," he told me. "You are beautiful. Special. You will come back to Iran, soon, and be who you were meant to be." Then, one night, after I told him I didn't know who I was meant to be anymore, he said to me, "My wife. Come back to Iran. And marry me."

I TOLD MY mother I had to return to Iran.

"For what?" she demanded.

"For Amir," I said. "He wants to marry me." I had nothing in Los Angeles. No job. No friends. I couldn't imagine what future America held for me. I wasn't a poet here or a revolutionary or an intellectual, or anything. I was an odd, reclusive young woman, frail and frightened, in a home among identical homes that stretched out eternally. *Maybe*, I thought, *if I returned to Tehran, maybe I could be, again, who I had been.* But I had no reason to explain my need to go back, other than the reason Amir offered me. And I thought to myself, *well, if nothing else, if I were wife to him, then I'd at least be something to somebody.*

Javid picked me up from Mehrabad International Airport and drove me back to my uncle's apartment. Sanam was already in the driveway, waiting. "Come in my car for a second," she said. "Let's take a drive and talk."

I had barely closed the door when she backed out screeching and drove past the mosque through the streets to a newly developed highway I had never seen, where she drove in the darkness with fierce resolve in her eyes. I was visibly broken. My shoulders hunched from the constant pain in the muscles of my upper body, the light in my eyes dimmed from the pain-killers, the sound of my voice dull. It must have been alarming to see such a sudden shift in someone's identity, and Sanam drove like she had to get me somewhere fast, to mend whatever she thought needed mending, to bring me back to what I was before I left Tehran.

"Where are we going?" I asked her.

"I just wanted to show you this new highway they're building, and talk."

Floodlights everywhere. Naked steel ribs sticking out every which way. The monstrous sleeping machines, cranes, rollers, diggers parked haphazardly on the sides. Scattered cones. No other cars.

"Are you supposed to drive on this highway?" I asked.

"They said it's open."

"And where does it lead?"

"A few towns."

"And which are we going to?"

"Nowhere, really."

". . ."

"You're with Amir now?"

"We've been talking on the phone."

"You came back for him?"

"I came back to be in Iran."

"He says you two are engaged."

". . ."

"Are you engaged to Amir?"

". . ."

"Why would you choose him? Why him?"

"He called, every night, Sanam. Leading up to my surgery. And after. It was real dark, for a while. He was a voice, the only voice sometimes, that got through in all that darkness."

"You can't marry him."

"Why not?"

"He isn't for you."

"Why isn't he?"

It was pretty late that night by the time Sanam pulled off that desolate highway into a quiet town, a more affluent one judging from the homes. She drove through wide, dark streets until she came to a fine wrought-iron gate. She jumped out of the car and pushed the button on the intercom. The gate slid open. A home. Modern. White concrete. A wall of windows. Warm light. And Ramin the photographer stood there in his wool cardigan with his hands deep in his pockets. "I brought you here to see him," Sanam said. "You two are meant for each other."

Ramin stood there, sheepish. The last time we had spoken was the phone conversation where I yelled at him about finding the fisherman, taking his photo, and stealing him from me. "You have to come out, you have to talk to him," Sanam said.

I was angry. Still. He was like the rest of them, the ones who had intruded into the depths of me and stolen what was mine. I got out of that car, slammed the door, walked toward Ramin. "Where's your phone?" I asked him. Without an embrace. Without a hello. Ramin led me into the house, to a room full of expensive postproduction equipment.

"My new boss's place," he said. "I'm in the middle of a big project."

I picked up the receiver and dialed Amir's number. And Amir picked up, as he always did, with that soothing, hypnotic voice.

"Where are you?" Amir asked.

"I don't know. Sanam drove me here, to see Ramin."

"Put her on the phone."

Twenty minutes later, Amir was in the driveway. He helped me into his car without a word to Sanam or to Ramin the photographer. I watched the both of them standing in the driveway, stark and despondent in the flood of Amir's headlights. Ramin turned and walked back into the home, but Sanam kept looking as we backed out.

"They don't understand you," Amir said. He placed his hand on my hand. It had been a long, long time since anybody had touched my body with ungloved hands. It felt cold, his touch. He squeezed my hand, looked at me, and smiled. "They don't know you the way I know you."

WHATEVER THE AIR was in Los Angeles, that thick foreboding, that heavy darkness, it had followed me. I walked the streets of Tehran in its haze. I saw the beggars, the prostitutes, the old women, the young. I saw the butchers, the police, the mullahs, the merchants. I heard the azaan rise from the minarets. I stood in the midst of it, searching for a glimpse of the beauty, for the tidal wave of love that washed over me when I was witness to the sublime hidden in plain view, and I saw nothing. I felt nothing.

Behrooz was sick. He had grown weaker. Pouya buried himself in work. Sarab invited me to his home, but I didn't have much poetry in me. Sanam refused to talk to me, and Ramin the photographer retreated completely. One night,

Amir sat in my room on the floor beside my bed. I told him I couldn't see anymore, that I had become blind. Amir leaned in and put his lips on my lips. His mouth a cold, dead thing. His tongue, rude. My body recoiled at his touch. I wanted to turn my face. To push him away. But I stepped away from my body, instead, the way I stepped away from my body that night in the parked car and, later, each time the doctors and nurses handled me. I thought to myself, *I don't feel any desire for this man. And since desire has led me to so much suffering, then its absence is the promise of safety.* So I let him kiss me.

Amir invited me to his home. Amir's mother was a homemaker and his father a bazaari. That's what that class of merchants were called in Iran. And they were notorious for being traditionalists. He came home each night to his warm dinner, ate his fill in silence, then, over the same bowl of vanilla ice cream, shared small talk with me and his family. They had a daughter, too, a good girl, a good student, pretty, and well liked. Amir was their darling, though. His parents gushed about his talents, his intelligence, his achievements, his lucrative career as an up-and-coming developer. Then, one evening after dinner with his family, Amir told me that he was ready to tell his parents about our plans. "You mean they don't know yet?" I asked him. "Who do they think I am, coming here so often?"

"My friend from America. I wanted them to know you first, before I tell them that we intend to marry."

The next afternoon, Amir called me in a panic.

"They found out that you have Jewish blood," he said. "I told them your father was Muslim, but they won't hear of it. My father wants to meet with you."

An hour later, I left my uncle's apartment to find them waiting in their car, Amir's dad behind the wheel, Amir beside him, deathly pale and silent. Amir's father did not invite me back to their home to speak in private. Instead, by chance, by some cosmic irony, he drove to the very neighborhood park my parents used to take me to as a child. The same slides, same swings, same trees. We walked to a bench beneath the sycamores. We sat there in silence for a few moments, Amir's father between us. The children on the playground laughed and screamed. Then, Amir's father spoke.

"My son has made a terrible mistake," he said. "He should have been clear with us about his relationship with you from the beginning. Because we would never have allowed him to continue pulling you along in such a fashion and wasting your time. But we are a traditional Iranian family, and this union is not in line with our traditions. We will not allow it."

I looked at Amir. He sat beside his father, hands clasped in his lap, looking down. I waited. Amir didn't say anything. His father watched me in turn. I looked back at Amir's father and said, "Your son loves me."

"That's not how it works here, my girl," Amir's father said. "Whether my son loves you or not has very little to do with this making a good marriage." Then he started to talk about tradition, about *our* ways, about roots and trees with roots and centuries of trees with roots, the longest extended metaphor of my life, really, as I waited for Amir to speak up to his father, to proclaim his love, to stand up to this man and say something. And Amir said nothing. He wouldn't even look at me.

"Amir?" I said.

He finally looked up. Lost. Wordless. *All those nights*, I wanted to yell, *you talked so brave, professed your undying love and your devotion and now, you have nothing to say to me?* But I didn't say that. I just looked at him, then I stood up from that park bench, turned to face his father and said, "Well, thank you both very much. I understand. And now, I must get going."

His father stood up, thrust out his chest, and said, "I will drive you back home."

"No," I said. "You will not."

"Of course I will. I brought you here, and I have an obligation to your family to return you safely them. It would be dishonorable of me to let you to walk home alone."

"Save your honor for yourself and your boy."

Then I walked. Away. In the general direction I thought might be my uncle's home.

Amir came running after me. "Please," he said. "Please, it's getting late. Let us drive you back?"

I ignored him and kept walking.

In that space, an indeterminable amount of time passed. I turned around and neither son nor father were anywhere to be seen. No evidence of them ever having been. I wondered for a moment if I had dreamed the whole thing. I stood on a street corner. It was dusk. Early summer. The sound of children playing. The long shadows of trees on the concrete. A young boy sat on his haunches nearby, fanning the coal in a portable barbeque, ears of corn roasting on it. He sang about his roasted, salted corn for sale. I could smell the smoke of the coal, the burning silk of corn. I stood there, listening to him, watching the cars pass on the street, and suddenly I was a young child again, standing on that very corner. My father had brought me here. But where was he? I looked around in panic. How would I ever find my way home without him?

I was terrified. I did not know where I stood. Which way to turn. I had no idea what had happened. Was I a child, lost at a park? Was I a young woman returned to the country of her origin to marry a man she did not love, and who did not have the courage to stand up for her? Were all those years I thought I had lived a moment in a child's reverie as she wandered away, unseen? Time contracted upon itself, and I was lost, completely. I stood on that street corner, and the only thing I knew for certain was that I didn't know the direction of home. I walked into a grocery store, and I must have been visibly distraught, because the clerk approached me and asked, "Are you all right?"

I remembered the name of our old street. "Please, can you tell me where to find Gheytarieh?"

He put his hand on my shoulder, gently led me to the door and into the street, to the corner, and said, "There, straight ahead. Would you like me to call you a cab?"

I wiped my tears, shook my head, and started walking. After a few blocks, I came to our old home, the apartment building of my childhood. I stood outside the gate that led to the long driveway into the parking garage below the building. I stood outside the gate and wondered why no one came for me. The sun set. The darkness. Then, I recalled a name. Sarab. A boy named Sarab. In that dream that may have been the life I had lived, he was my friend. He lived in a building on this same street, which I had left behind as a child, when my family fled to America. I found that building. I remembered a number, I pressed it on the intercom. Raya, his mother, answered, her voice crackling through.

"It's me," I said.

"Why are you here at this late hour?" She asked. "Come up."

The buzz.

The stairs.

That open door.

Raya mixed some herb concoction in a glass of water with sugar and ice. She called Behrooz and told him I was safe, not to worry. Then she asked me, gently, "What happened? What did you see that's shaken you up like this? You look like you've seen a ghost."

I had seen a ghost.

I had seen the ghost of myself. I saw her, mute, broken by the touch of a man she had once loved. I saw her torn open, manipulated, fixed, sewn back up by hands of strangers. I saw her sitting in a room, watching the shadows creep along the walls, day after day, afraid to move, afraid to feel. I saw this ghost of me, sitting on a park bench, ready to walk into a life empty of desire, of longing. And I had stood up and walked away from her. Left her behind. With the ghost of those two men, and all the others in the past, all the ones who had been.

ON A HOT day in midsummer, with the passenger window rolled down and the breeze sweeping my scarf off my head, I rested my arm on the ledge of the car window. I leaned away from Amir, focused on my own hand instead, outlined gold by the sun I blocked with my palm. I watched the world pass through my outspread fingers, winding green mountains, deep chasms, gorges lush and teeming with forests, rivers mad with torrents, encampments of picnicking families. We drove by the occasional roadside storefront where inflatable super-heroes, bunched together, hung from string over glass bottles of soda baking in the sun. Old men, sitting in plastic chairs next to crates of apples, stared back at me. Children stood beside the road, faces dust-covered, waving. I waved back, my chin resting on my arm, my hair revealed.

The night after our meeting in the park, Amir's father had turned purple, gasped for breath, fell to the floor clutching his chest in pain. Amir's mother called me on the phone the next day, weeping, and begged me to leave Iran and return to America. His sister called, too, crying that I was tearing apart her family. But it took two weeks before Amir, himself, called me. "They want to report you to Intelligence. They want to accuse you of trying to convert me to Judaism," he said. "That's a death sentence. For you. But don't worry, I have stopped eating. Soon, they will listen to me."

Behrooz and his wife had left Tehran for Paris to see a renowned neurologist in hope of finding an answer. Javid and Pouya were never home. I sat alone in that apartment, in Tehran. Strange men started coming to the door in the after-noons and evenings. They rang from downstairs to ask if I had called for a cab, if I had ordered an electrician, if so-and-so lived at that address. Amir wouldn't call for days and days, then he'd call, whispering into the phone, "I am making progress with them, please be patient a bit longer."

Sarab invited me to stay in a cottage by the Caspian Sea with his band. Amir decided it was the perfect opportunity to come see me. He lied to his parents about where he was going, then drove in the dead of night. I waited in the attic bedroom of that cottage, in the dim light of a single light bulb that hung over a wrought iron bed, beside a window that looked out to the dark sea. I heard him arrive, greet the boys, walk up the narrow, winding stairs. I did not turn to look at him when he walked into that room and fell to his knees before me, weeping.

I opened my eyes the next day to find Amir already awake. Outside, the sea beckoned and, somewhere, in all that expanse, there might have been a red boat. The sunlight flooded through the attic window in a stream of gold. Dust motes danced in it. He was handsome in that morning light, his dark hair mussed, his lean body outlined beneath the white sheet. I turned away from him.

"You are so beautiful," he said.

"Let's go."

"Let's never go back."

I didn't say goodbye to the boys. I threw my backpack in the backseat of Amir's car, sat in the passenger side, rolled down the window, and waited while he said goodbye to Sarab, Shervin, and the rest. They spoke and looked in my direction with worry, but I looked away. Amir drove us out of the seaside town. "Let's go somewhere, together. Another city. Shiraz, maybe. Or Isfahan," he said.

"What will you say to your parents?"

"That I needed to take a long drive and be alone, to think things through."

"Take me back to Tehran."

"Give me time, please," he said. "I will persuade them." The road narrowed, the curves sharpening so that we couldn't see what was coming until the car turned the bend. We sat in silence for much of the drive.

Then I heard the men's voices. Someone shouted a phrase, and a chorus of men chanted the refrain back. The sound of heavy boots on asphalt. A pounding. I leaned my head out of the window to see and when we turned the bend, we found ourselves suddenly driving amidst hundreds of young soldiers who were jogging up that mountainous road, rifles on their shoulders, beneath the blazing sun.

Amir had to slow the car to a crawl, then to a near stop. We were in a sea of men in green, dust-covered fatigues. I did not readjust my headscarf to hide my hair. I did not sit back in my seat and roll up my window. I looked at them. And in the crowd of all those boys, one young soldier stopped jogging and looked right back at me. The sunlight shone on him, alone, like a spotlight, like some holy illumination cast by heaven, and I knew, among all those soldiers, this one. And he, too, recognized something in me.

Perhaps it is the evolution of genome recognition, that what I needed, that one young soldier had, and what he needed, I had, so that we could create the optimal offspring. Perhaps chance. Perhaps the right timing in both of our circadian rhythms. Or an alignment of stars, the phase of the moon, the currents of the nearby sea. Perhaps, within me, an aching emptiness, and within him the need to expel some hidden longing. Perhaps the illusion of familiarity. Or a molecular truth too invisible to comprehend. Or a truth just beyond molecules and comprehension.

He was tall with a face etched in stone. Eyes alive, clear. Face glistening with sweat. Full lips parted with heavy breath. Golden. He looked at me with brutal, open desire. And I looked back and felt a brutal and forgotten longing. All those men, marching, singing, tired, sweating, black boots, shaved heads. I leaned out of my window among them and wanted to reach my hand in his direction. I wanted to touch his shoulder, his arm, the sweat-drenched uniform that stretched tight across his chest. A voice in my head warned *this will only lead to more pain.* And something in me screamed back, *he is burning with life and I, too, I, too, am still burning.*

Amir glanced in my direction. I could feel his eyes on me. I unbuckled my seat belt, got to my knees, and leaned my entire upper body out of that window as Amir drove slowly through the crowd of those men. I stared at that soldier, unashamed. And he stared back, unashamed. And the distance between that soldier and me was less than the distance that had been between my body and Amir's the night before in that attic bedroom, even though Amir's hand touched the raised black scar beneath my breast, even though his promises had fallen on the nape of my neck. In the infinitesimal moment as the car inched through the crowd of men, a thousand nights passed between that soldier and me.

The car finally turned the next bend, and the road before us stretched empty. All that remained was the sound of their boots, the chorus of their voices growing fainter. Amir cleared his throat and said something about me sitting back down. I leaned farther out of my window and looked down into the chasm that yawned past the precipice of that narrow mountainous road. Amir said something more, but I could not hear him for the wind. I inhaled deeply, and in that breath, the whole of the world filled me.

Dear Behrooz,

I am flying over New Orleans on my way to the East Coast for a reading. Below this airplane is a city flooded with music, with sorrow and joy and suffering and all that makes humanity so beautiful. And somewhere above this city, beyond this airplane, in the thin atmosphere, you exist. An infinite, or finite, number of particles mixed with ice and pollen and the dispersed atoms of dragonflies.

Dear Behrooz,

Earth has been lonely without you. The stars dim. The city lights dwindling. And the mountains . . . I drove up to the top of one and looked across to the others that sat, infinitely patient, watching the oceans come and go, dressed in tall redwood trees, draping mist about their shoulders, and I looked to their crowns and thought, *how impossible to walk down this mountain and up another through the tangle of trees, in the direction of ocean, to climb the steep side and reach the summit. How impossible.* And the mountains responded with silence.

And then I remembered what you taught me, that it begins with a step and is followed by another and the summit is no glory of its own, but that it is all glory, each step past the fear of cold death, and every little lichen clinging to a rock, each salamander hidden beneath a rotting log.

Listen, I began writing this note to tell you what I just learned from a tangerine. It is winter now and almost two decades have passed from when I walked behind you, up those paths to the summits of all that glory. Autumns have come and gone, come and gone. It is the season of tangerine. I peeled one just now. I brought it close to my face and I pulled off its skin, which slid off easily. The droplets, as tiny as dust, burst between its skin and flesh so that its perfume filled the whole cabin and I had to close my eyes at that point, so that I wouldn't see the other passengers and feel ashamed for taking such pleasure in public. I inhaled and held the soft, supple globe of that fruit, and it gave itself to me, a perfect sliver of itself, and I knew, before placing it in my mouth, I knew its feeble pretense, the coy tautness of its skin before those hundred little globules would give between my teeth.

I had a dream a few weeks back that I sat inside a tomb, and there was a small piece of cake before me, and I took a forkful of it and ate and I knew there must be pleasure, but I couldn't taste anything. So I took another bite, searching, knowing there must be texture and taste to crumb and cream. But I felt nothing. Because the mind alone cannot taste. Because the body, Behrooz, the body knows texture and tastes. The body is born to feel the world, to know it through the tongue, the fingers, the nose, eyes, ears, the fine hairs on the surface of the skin.

And what then, without a body? What becomes of the tangerine? What becomes of the world and all its beauty? When you are particles smaller than pollen, frailer than ice, high above this filthy, beautiful Earth, when you dissipate into heaven, formless, what becomes of all that longing?

Now there is nothing below this plane but the black waters of the Gulf of Mexico. No lights. No cities. No mountains.

Just dark waters and whatever glitters beneath their secret folds.

ACKNOWLEDGMENTS

I AM INDEBTED to Leigh Feldman, whose faith in my work has pulled me through some dark, dark hours. To Cassandra Farrin and Dayna Anderson, for their courage. To Cherrita Lee, for picking up the pieces. To my cousins and their families. To my late uncle Behrooz and his wife, for taking me in and showing me the world. To the friends I mention in this book, and to the others I cannot, but who have stayed in my heart, still, and inspire me, always. To my mother, to my husband, to my family. To my daughters, who are my everything. And to the beautiful people of Iran, who welcomed this stranger and helped her find home.

ABOUT THE AUTHOR

PARNAZ FOROUTAN is the author of *The Girl from the Garden* (Ecco 2015). She currently lives in a suburb of Los Angeles.

ABOUT THE AUTHOR

PARNAZ FOROUTAN is the author of *The Girl from the Garden* (Ecco 2015). She currently lives in a suburb of Los Angeles.